CBEST California Basic Educational Skills Test

Teacher Certification Exam

By: Sharon Wynne, M.S.
Southern Connecticut State University

"And, while there's no reason yet to panic, I think it's only prudent that we make preparations to panic."

XAMonline, INC.

Boston

To obtain permission(s) to use the material from this work for any purpose including workshops or seminars, please submit a written request to:

XAMonline, Inc.
21 Orient Ave.
Melrose, MA 02176
Toll Free 1-800-509-4128
Email: info@xamonline.com
Web: www.xamonline.com
Fax: 1-781-662-9268

Library of Congress Cataloging-in-Publication Data

Wynne, Sharon A.
     CBEST: California Basic Educational Skills Test: Teacher Certification / Sharon A. Wynne.
     ISBN: 978-1-58197-596-3
          1. CBEST: California Basic Educational Skills Test   2. Study Guides
          3. CBEST   4. Teachers Certification & Licensure   5. Careers

Disclaimer:

The opinions expressed in this publication are the sole works of XAMonline and were created independently from the National Education Association, Educational Testing Service, or any State Department of Education, National Evaluation Systems or other testing affiliates.

Between the time of publication and printing, state specific standards as well as testing formats and website information may change and those potential changes are not addressed in part or in whole within this product. Sample test questions are developed by XAMonline and reflect content similar to that found on real tests; however, they are not former tests. XAMonline assembles content that aligns with state standards but does not guarantee that teacher candidates will achieve passing score. Numerical scores are determined by testing companies such as NES or ETS and then are compared with individual state standards. A passing score varies from state to state.

Printed in the United States of America   œ-1

CBEST: California Basic Educational Skills Test
ISBN: 978-1-58197-596-3

TEACHER CERTIFICATION STUDY GUIDE

Table of Contents

SUBAREA I.   **READING**

COMPETENCY 1.0   **CRITICAL ANALYSIS AND EVALUATION** 1

Skill 1.1   Compare/contrast ideas or information presented in different sections of a reading selection or from different sources 1

Skill 1.2   Identify the reasons, examples, details, or facts in a reading selection that support the author's main idea 2

Skill 1.3   Make predictions about the outcome of an event based on information from a reading selection 3

Skill 1.4   Recognize the attitude, opinion, or viewpoint expressed by the author toward his or her subject 5

Skill 1.5   Determine whether facts or ideas are relevant to an argument in a reading selection 7

Skill 1.6   Recognize statements that strengthen or weaken arguments in a reading selection 8

Skill 1.7   Recognize the various persuasive techniques used by an author in a reading selection 10

Skill 1.8   Distinguish between facts and opinions in a reading selection 11

Skill 1.9   Challenge the statements and opinions presented in a reading selection 12

Skill 1.10   Identify inconsistencies or differences in points of view within one reading selection or between two or more selections 14

Skill 1.11   Recognize the audience that a reading selection addresses 15

Skill 1.12   Recognize language that creates an inappropriate or inconsistent tone, given the intended audience and purpose 16

COMPETENCY 2.0   COMPREHENSION AND CONTEXT 17

Skill 2.1   Identify the relationships between general and specific ideas in a reading selection 17

Skill 2.2   Determine the sequence of events or steps in a process from a reading selection 17

Skill 2.3   Arrange the ideas in a reading selection into an outline or another form of graphic organization 18

Skill 2.4   Recognize the main idea or purpose of a reading selection 19

Skill 2.5   Identify accurate paraphrases or summaries of ideas in a reading selection 20

Skill 2.6   Identify facts and details presented in a reading selection 20

Skill 2.7   Draw conclusions or generalizations from material presented in a reading selection 20

Skill 2.8   Make inferences and recognize implications based on information from a reading selection 21

Skill 2.9   Recognize implied relationships between people, ideas, or events in a reading selection 21

Skill 2.10   Use context clues, syntax, and structural analysis to determine the meaning of unknown words 22

Skill 2.11   Determine the meanings of figurative or colloquial language in a reading selection 26

Skill 2.12   Recognize and identify different interpretations that can be made of the same word, sentence, paragraph, or reading selection 28

Skill 2.13   Recognize how the meaning of a word, sentence, or paragraph is affected by the context in which it appears 28

Skill 2.14   Understand the function of key transition indicators in a reading selection 29

COMPETENCY 3.0   RESEARCH AND REFERENCE SKILLS.................... 31

Skill 3.1   Use the table of contents, section headings, index, and similar sections of a book to locate information 31

Skill 3.2   Locate the place in a reading selection where a specific kind of information can be found 31

Skill 3.3   Understand how a reading selection is organized 31

Sample Test: Reading 33

Answer Key: Reading 46

Rigor Table: Reading 47

Rationales for Sample Questions: Reading 48

SUBAREA II.   MATHEMATICS

COMPETENCY 4.0   ESTIMATION AND MEASUREMENT........................74

Skill 4.1   Understand and use standard units of length, temperature, weight, and capacity in the U.S. measurement system 74

Skill 4.2   Measure length and perimeter 76

Skill 4.3   Understand and use estimates of time to plan and achieve work-related objectives 84

Skill 4.4   Estimate the results of problems involving addition, subtraction, multiplication, and division prior to computation 85

COMPETENCY 5.0   STATISTICAL PRINCIPLES.......................................87

Skill 5.1   Perform arithmetic operations with basic statistical data related to test scores 87

Skill 5.2   Understand basic principles of probability and predict likely outcomes based on data provided....:..91

Skill 5.3   Interpret the meaning of standardized test scores to determine how individuals performed relative to other students 94

COMPETENCY 6.0   COMPUTATION & PROBLEM SOLVING 96

Skill 6.1   Add, subtract, multiply, and divide with whole numbers 96

Skill 6.2   Add and subtract with positive and negative numbers 101

Skill 6.3   Add, subtract, multiply, and divide with fractions, decimals, and percentages 102

Skill 6.4   Determine and perform necessary arithmetic operations to solve a practical mathematics problem...110

Skill 6.5   Solve simple algebraic problems...110

Skill 6.6   Determine whether enough information is given to solve a problem; identify the facts given in a problem 112

Skill 6.7   Recognize alternative mathematical methods of solving a problem 113

COMPETENCY 7.0   NUMERICAL & GRAPHIC RELATIONSHIPS............116

Skill 7.1   Recognize relationships in numerical data.................................116

Skill 7.2   Recognize the position of numbers in relation to each other.........117

Skill 7.3   Use the relations *less than*, *greater than*, or *equal to*, and their associated symbols to express a numerical relationship...............120

Skill 7.4   Identify numbers, formulas, and mathematical expressions that are mathematically equivalent..121

Skill 7.5   Understand and use rounding rules when solving problems..........123

Skill 7.6   Understand and apply the meaning of logical connectives and quantifiers 126

Skill 7.7   Identify or specify a missing entry from a table of data 129

Skill 7.8   Use numerical information contained in tables, spreadsheets, and various kinds of graphs to solve mathematics problems................130

Sample Test: Mathematics...133

Answer Key: Mathematics 148

Rigor Table: Mathematics 149

Rationales for Sample Questions: Mathematics 150

SUBAREA III.   WRITING

COMPETENCY 8.0   WRITING THE ESSAY 185

Great Study and Testing Tips!

What to study in order to prepare for the subject assessments is the focus of this study guide, but equally important is *how* you study.

You can increase your chances of truly mastering the information by taking some simple, but effective, steps.

Study Tips:

1. <u>Some foods aid the learning process</u>. Foods such as milk, nuts, seeds, rice, and oats help your study efforts by releasing natural memory enhancers called CCKs (*cholecystokinin*) composed of *tryptophan*, *choline*, and *phenylalanine*. All of these chemicals enhance the neurotransmitters associated with memory. Before studying, try a light, protein-rich meal of eggs, turkey, and fish. All of these foods release the memory enhancing chemicals. The better the connections, the more you comprehend.

Likewise, before you take a test, stick to a light snack of energy-boosting and relaxing foods. A glass of milk, a piece of fruit, or some peanuts all release various memory-boosting chemicals and help you to relax and focus on the subject at hand.

2. <u>Learn to take great notes</u>. A by-product of our modern culture is that we have grown accustomed to getting our information in short doses (i.e. TV news sound bites or USA Today style newspaper articles).

Consequently, we've subconsciously trained ourselves to assimilate information better in <u>neat little packages</u>. If your notes are scrawled all over the paper, then the flow of the information gets fragmented. Strive for clarity. Newspapers use a standard format to achieve clarity. Your notes can be much clearer through use of proper formatting. A very effective format is called the <u>*"Cornell Method."*</u>

> Take a sheet of loose-leaf lined notebook paper, and draw a line all the way down the paper about 1-2″ from the left-hand edge.

> Draw another line across the width of the paper about 1-2″ up from the bottom. Repeat this process on the reverse side of the page.

Look at the highly effective result. You have ample room for notes, a left hand margin for special emphasis items or for inserting supplementary data from the textbook, a large area at the bottom for a brief summary, and a little rectangular space for just about anything you want.

3. <u>**Get the concept, then the details**</u>. Too often we focus on the details and don't gather an understanding of the concept. However, if we simply memorize only dates, places, or names, we may well miss the whole point of the subject.

A key way to understand things is to put them in your own words. If you are working from a textbook, automatically summarize each paragraph in your mind. If you are outlining text, don't simply copy the author's words.

Rephrase them in your own words (paraphrase). You remember your own thoughts and words much better than someone else's and subconsciously tend to associate the important details to the core concepts.

4. <u>**Ask Why?**</u> Pull apart written material paragraph by paragraph, and don't forget the captions under the illustrations.

Example: If the heading is "Stream Erosion," flip it around to read, "Why do streams erode?" Then answer the questions.

If you train your mind to think in a series of questions and answers, not only will you learn more, but you will experience less test anxiety because you are used to answering questions.

5. <u>**Read for reinforcement and future needs**</u>. Even if you only have 10 minutes, put your notes or a book in your hand. Your mind is similar to a computer; you have to input data in order to have it processed. *By reading, you are creating neural connections for future retrieval.* The more times you read something, the more you reinforce the learning of ideas.

Even if you don't fully understand something on the first pass, *your mind stores much of the material for later recall.*

6. <u>**Relax to learn, and go into exile**</u>. Our bodies respond to an inner clock comprised of biorhythms. Burning the midnight oil works well for some people, but it's not for everyone.

If possible, set aside a particular place to study that is free from distractions. Shut off the television, cell phone, and pager, and exile your friends and family during your study period.

If you really are bothered by silence, try background music. Light classical music at a low volume has been shown to promote concentration more than other types of music. Music that evokes pleasant emotions without lyrics is highly suggested. Just about anything by Mozart will relax you.

7. <u>**Use arrows, not highlighters**</u>. At best, it's difficult to read a page full of yellow, pink, blue, and green streaks. Try staring at a neon sign for a while, and you'll soon

see that the horde of colors obscures the message. A quick note, a brief dash of color, an underline, and an arrow pointing to a particular passage are much clearer than a horde of highlighted words.

8. **Budget your study time.** Although you shouldn't ignore any of the material, *allocate your available study time in the same ratio that topics are likely to appear on the test.*

Testing Tips:

1. **Get smart, play dumb. Don't read anything into the question.** Don't make an assumption that the test writer is looking for something else than what is asked. Stick to the question as written, and don't read extra things into it.

2. **Read the question and all the choices *twice* before answering the question.** You may miss something by not carefully reading, and then re-reading, both the question and the answers.

If you really don't have a clue as to the right answer, leave it blank on the first time through. Go on to the other questions because they may provide a clue as to how to answer the skipped question.

If later on, you still can't answer the skipped ones . . . ***Guess.*** The only penalty for guessing is that you *might* get them wrong. Only one thing is certain; if you don't put anything down, you will get them wrong!

3. **Turn the question into a statement.** Look at the way the questions are worded. The syntax of the question usually provides a clue. Does it seem more familiar as a statement rather than as a question? Does it sound strange?

By turning a question into a statement, you may be able to spot if an answer sounds right, and doing so may also trigger memories of material that you have read.

4. **Look for hidden clues.** It's actually very difficult to compose multiple-foil (choice) questions without giving away part of the answer in the options presented.

In most multiple-choice questions, you can often readily eliminate one or two of the potential answers. This leaves you with only two real possibilities, and automatically your odds increase to fifty-fifty.

5. **Trust your instincts.** For every fact that you have read, you subconsciously retain something of that knowledge. On questions that you aren't really certain about, go with your basic instincts. **Your first impression of how to answer a question is usually correct.**

6. **Mark your answers directly on the test booklet.** Don't bother trying to fill in the optical scan sheet on the first pass through the test.

Be careful not to miss-mark your answers when you transcribe them to the scan sheet.

7. **Watch the clock!** You have a set amount of time to answer the questions. Don't get bogged down trying to answer a single question at the expense of 10 questions you can more readily answer.

THIS PAGE BLANK

COMPETENCY 1.0   CRITICAL ANALYSIS AND EVALUATION

Skill 1.1   Compare/contrast ideas or information presented in different sections of a reading selection or from different sources

To **compare** ideas or pieces of information presented in different sections of a reading selection or from different sources is to point out the similarities between or among such ideas or pieces of information. To **contrast** such ideas or pieces of information is to point out the differences between or among them.

Keeping track of how the different sections of a reading selection or how different sources present similar or differing ideas or pieces of information reinforces those ideas for the reader (comparing) or alerts readers that there is some degree of controversy operative in the discussion (contrasting). It might even reveal weaknesses, errors, or inconsistencies in the author's or authors' presentation(s). Both activities, comparing and contrasting, are active reading skills. This means that they require readers to engage with text beyond merely decoding the words in the immediate context. Both activities promote better understanding of the text(s) and longer retention of the information.

Using **graphic organizers** to track comparisons and contrasts can help readers gain a clearer understanding of the points that the author has (or authors have) in mind. Venn diagrams are graphic organizers particularly suited to track comparisons and contrasts. A Venn diagram has two circles, each circle representing ideas or information from a particular section of a reading selection or from a particular source, and these circles are drawn so that there is an overlap area common to both. Similarities (comparisons) between the ideas or information from the two sections or sources are recorded in the overlap area of the Venn diagram, and differences (contrasts) are recorded in the other areas of the two circles.

As an example of how to apply comparison and contrast skills, consider Edgar Allen Poe's short story, "The Tell-Tale Heart." In it, Poe employed first person narration to describe a bizarre murder and its after-effects on the narrator, the guilty party. At the beginning of the story, the narrator stated that his purpose in describing the events was to establish that he was not crazy because he could describe them impassively. As he nears the story's end, his descriptions become far from impassive.

By contrasting his promise to tell the story impassively with his later wild description of events, readers can gain the insight needed to conclude that, even by his own minimal standards, the narrator was truly crazy. Another useful application of these skills to the same story could be to compare how nearly every paragraph of the story included at least one revelation by the narrator that would tend to establish that he was crazy no matter how calmly he could tell the story. Both applications allow readers to gain insight into the story's real point.

Skill 1.2   Identify the reasons, examples, details, or facts in a reading selection that support the author's main idea

Supporting details are examples, facts, ideas, illustrations, cases, and anecdotes used by a writer to explain, expand on, and develop the more general main idea. A writer's choice of supporting materials is determined by the nature of the topic being covered. Supporting details are specifics that relate directly to the main idea. Writers select and shape material according to their purposes. An advertisement writer seeking to persuade readers to buy a particular running shoe, for instance, will emphasize only the positive characteristics of the shoe in advertisement copy. A columnist for a running magazine, on the other hand, might list the good and bad points about the same shoe in an article recommending appropriate shoes for different kind of runners. Both major details (those that directly support the main idea) and minor details (those that provide interesting, but not always essential, information) help create a well-written and fluid passage.

In the following paragraph, the sentences in **bold print** provide a skeleton of a paragraph on the benefits of recycling. The sentences in **bold** are generalizations that, by themselves, do not explain the need to recycle. The sentences in *italics* add details to show the general points in bold. Notice how the supporting details help you understand the necessity for recycling.

While one day recycling may become mandatory in all states, right now it is voluntary in many communities. *Those of us who participate in recycling are amazed by how much material is recycled.* **For many communities, the blue-box recycling program has had an immediate effect.** *By just recycling glass, aluminum cans, and plastic bottles, we have reduced the volume of disposable trash by one third, thus extending the useful life of local landfills by over a decade. Imagine the difference if those dramatic results were achieved nationwide.* **The amount of reusable items we thoughtlessly dispose of is staggering.** *For example, Americans dispose of enough steel every day to supply Detroit car manufacturers for three months. Additionally, we dispose of enough aluminum annually to rebuild the nation's air fleet. These statistics, available from the Environmental Protection Agency (EPA), should encourage all of us to watch what we throw away.* **Clearly, recycling in our homes and in our communities directly improves the environment.**

Notice how the author's supporting examples enhance the message of the paragraph and relate to the thesis noted above. If you only read the boldface sentences, you have a glimpse of the topic. This paragraph of illustration, however, is developed through numerous details creating specific images: *reduced the volume of disposable trash by one-third; extended the useful life of local landfills by over a decade; enough steel everyday to supply Detroit car manufacturers for three months; enough aluminum to rebuild the nation's air fleet.* If the writer had merely written a few general sentences, then you would not fully understand the vast amount of trash involved in recycling or the positive results of current recycling efforts.

Skill 1.3   Make predictions about the outcome of an event based on information from a reading selection

An **inference** is sometimes called an "educated guess" because it requires that you go beyond the strictly obvious to create additional meaning by taking the text one logical step further. Inferences and conclusions are based on the content of the passage – that is, on what the passage says or how the writer says it – and are derived by reasoning.

Inference is an essential and automatic component of most reading. For example, it is operative in determining the meaning of unknown words, the authors' main ideas, or whether or not authors have a bias. Such is the essence of inference: you use your own ability to reason in order to figure out what writers imply. As a reader, then, you must often logically extend your thinking in order to understand what authors only imply.

Consider the following example. Assume that you are an employer and that you are reading over the letters of reference submitted by a prospective employee for the position of clerk/typist in your real estate office. The position requires the applicant to be neat, careful, trustworthy, and punctual. You come across this letter of reference submitted by an applicant:

To whom it may concern,

Todd Finley has asked me to write a letter of reference for him. I am well qualified to do so because he worked for me for three months last year. His duties included answering the phone, greeting the public, and producing some simple memos and notices on the computer. Although Todd initially had few computer skills and little knowledge of telephone etiquette, he did acquire some during his stay with us. Todd's manner of speaking, both on the telephone and with the clients who came to my establishment, could be described as casual. He was particularly effective when communicating with peers. Please contact me by telephone if you wish to have further information about my experience.

Here the writer implies, rather than openly states, the main idea. This letter calls attention to itself because there's a problem with its tone. A truly positive letter would say something like "I have the distinct honor of recommending Todd Finley." Here, however, the letter simply verifies that Todd worked in the office. Second, the praise is obviously lukewarm. For example, the writer says that Todd "was particularly effective when communicating with peers." An educated guess translates that statement into a nice way of saying that Todd was not serious enough in his communications with clients.

In order to draw **inferences** and come to **conclusions**, a reader must use prior knowledge and apply it to the current situation. A conclusion is rarely, and an inference is never, stated. You must rely on your inferential skills to apprehend them.

Practice Questions: Read the following passages and select an answer.

1. Tim Sullivan had just turned 15. As a birthday present, his parents had given him a guitar and a certificate for 10 guitar lessons. He had always shown a love of music and a desire to learn an instrument. Tim began his lessons, and, before long, he was making up his own songs. At the music studio, Tim met Josh, who played the piano, and Roger, whose instrument was the saxophone. They all shared the same dream of starting a band, and each was praised by his teacher as having real talent.

    From this passage one can infer that

    A. Tim, Roger & Josh are going to start their own band.
    B. Tim is going to give up his guitar lessons.
    C. Tim, Josh & Roger will no longer be friends.
    D. Josh & Roger are going to start their own band.

2. The Smith family waited patiently around Carousel Number 7 for their luggage to arrive. They were exhausted after their 5-hour trip and were anxious to get to their hotel. After about an hour, they realized that they no longer recognized any of the other passengers' faces. Mrs. Smith asked the person who appeared to be in charge if they were at the right carousel. The man replied, "Yes, this is it, but we finished unloading that baggage almost half an hour ago."

    From the man's response we can infer that:

    A. The Smiths were ready to go to their hotel.
    B. The Smiths' luggage was lost.
    C. The man had their luggage.
    D. They were at the wrong carousel.

Answers:

1. (A) is the correct choice. Given the facts that Tim wanted to be a musician and start his own band, after meeting others who shared the same dreams, Tim probably joined them in an attempt to make their dreams become reality.

2. Since the Smiths were still waiting for their luggage, we know that they were not yet ready to go to their hotel. From the man's response, we know that they were not at the wrong carousel and that he did not have their luggage. Therefore, though not directly stated, it appears that their luggage was lost. Choice (B) is the correct answer.

Skill 1.4	Recognize the attitude, opinion, or viewpoint expressed by the authors toward their topics

An essay is an extended discussion of a writer's point of view about a particular topic. This point of view may be supported by using such writing modes as example, argument and persuasion, analysis, or comparison/contrast. In any case, a good essay is clear, coherent, well-organized, and fully developed.

When authors set out to write a passage, they usually have a purpose for doing so. That purpose may be to simply give information that might be interesting or useful to readers; it may be to persuade readers of a point of view or to move them to act in a particular way; it may be to tell a story; or it may be to describe something in such a way that an experience becomes available to readers through one or more of the five senses. Following are the primary devices for expressing a particular purpose in a piece of writing:

Basic expository writing simply gives information not previously known about a topic or is used to explain or define one. Facts, examples, statistics, cause and effect, direct tone, objective rather than subjective delivery, and non-emotional information are presented in a formal manner.

- **Descriptive writing** centers on person, place, or object using concrete and sensory words to create a mood or impression and arranges details in a chronological or spatial sequence.

- **Narrative writing** is developed using an incident, an anecdote, or a related series of events. Chronology, the 5 W's, topic sentence, and conclusion are essential ingredients.

- **Persuasive writing** implies a writer's ability to select vocabulary and to arrange facts and opinions in such a way that readers are moved to accept some target position. Persuasive writing may incorporate exposition and narration in pursuit of the main persuasive goal.

- **Journalistic writing** is theoretically free of author bias. It is essential when relaying information about an event, person, or thing that the information be factual and objective. Provide students with an opportunity to examine newspapers and to create their own. Many newspapers have educational programs that offer free papers to schools.

The **tone** of a written passage refers to an author's attitude toward the subject matter. The tone (mood, feeling) is revealed through such stylistic elements as vocabulary choice and sentence structure. The tone of the written passage is much like a speaker's voice; instead of being spoken, however, it is the product of words on a page.

Often, writers have an emotional stake in the subject; and their purpose, either explicitly or implicitly, is to convey those feelings to the reader. In such cases, the writing is generally subjective: that is, it stems from opinions, judgments, values, ideas, and feelings. Both sentence structure (syntax) and word choice (diction) are instrumental tools in creating tone.

Tone may be thought of generally as positive, negative, or neutral. Below is a statement about snakes that demonstrates this.

> *Many species of snakes live in California. Some of those species, both poisonous and non-poisonous, share habitats with humans.*

The voice of the writer in this statement is neutral. The sentences are declarative (not exclamations, fragments, or questions). The adjectives are few and nondescript—*many, some, poisonous* (balanced with *non-poisonous*). Nothing much in this brief paragraph would alert the reader to the feelings of the writer about snakes. The paragraph has a neutral, objective, detached, impartial tone.

If the writer's attitude toward snakes involves admiration or even affection, the tone would generally be positive:

> *California snakes are a tenacious bunch. When they find their habitats invaded by humans, they cling to their home territories as long as they can, as if vainly attempting to fight off the onslaught of the human hordes.*

An additional message emerges in this paragraph: The writer quite clearly favors snakes over people. The writer uses positive adjectives like *tenacious* to describe the snakes. The writer also humanizes the reptiles, making them seem to be brave, beleaguered creatures. Obviously, the writer is more sympathetic to snakes than to people in this paragraph.

If the writer's attitude toward snakes involves active dislike and fear, then the tone would also reflect that attitude by being negative:

> *Countless species of snakes, some more dangerous than others, still lurk on the urban fringes of California's towns and cities. They will often invade domestic spaces, terrorizing people and their pets.*

Here, obviously, the snakes are the villains. They *lurk,* they *invade,* and they *terrorize.* The tone of this paragraph might be said to be distressed about snakes. In the same manner, a writer can use language to portray characters as good or bad. A writer uses positive and negative adjectives, as seen above, to express what a character is like.

Skill 1.5   Determine whether facts or ideas are relevant to an argument in a reading selection

The main idea of a passage may contain a wide variety of supporting information, but it is important that each sentence be related to the main idea. When a sentence contains information that bears little or no connection to the main idea, it is said to be **irrelevant**. It is important to continually assess whether or not a sentence contributes to the overall task of supporting the main idea. When a sentence is deemed irrelevant, it is best to either omit it from the passage or to make it relevant by one of the following strategies:

1. Adding detail – Sometimes a sentence can seem out of place if it does not contain enough information to link it to the topic. Adding specific information can show how the sentence relates to the main idea.

2. Adding an example – This is especially important in passages in which information is being argued, compared, or contrasted. Examples can support the main idea and give the document overall credibility.

3. Using diction effectively – When selecting words, it is important to understand connotation, avoid ambiguity, and avoid too much repetition.

4. Adding transitions – Transitions are extremely helpful for making sentences relevant because they are specifically designed to connect one idea to another. They can also reduce choppiness.

The following passage has several irrelevant sentences that are highlighted in bold.

The New City Planning Committee is proposing a new capitol building to represent the multicultural face of New City. **The current mayor is a Democrat.** The new capitol building will be on 10th Street across from the grocery store and next to the Recreational Center. It will be within walking distance to the subway and bus depot because the designers want to emphasize the importance of public transportation. Aesthetically, the building will have a contemporary design featuring a brushed-steel exterior and large, floor-to-ceiling windows. **It is important for employees to have a connection with the outside world even when they are in their offices.** Inside the building, the walls will be moveable. This will not only facilitate a multitude of creative floor plans, but it will also create a focus on open communication and on smooth flow of information. **It sounds a bit gimmicky to me.** Finally, the capitol will feature a large outdoor courtyard full of lush greenery and serene fountains. **Work will now seem like Club Med to those who work at the New City capitol!**

Skill 1.6   Recognize statements that strengthen or weaken arguments in a reading selection

An argument is a generalization that is proven or supported with facts. If the facts are not accurate, the generalization remains unproven. Using inaccurate "facts" to support an argument creates a *fallacy* in the overall reasoning. Some factors to consider in judging whether the facts used to support an argument are accurate are as follows:

1. Are the facts current, or are they out of date? For example, if the proposition "birth defects in babies born to drug-using mothers are increasing," then the data must include the latest that is available.
2. Another important factor to consider in judging the accuracy of a fact is its source. Where were the data obtained, and is that source reliable?
3. The calculations on which the facts are based may be unreliable. It's a good idea to run one's own calculations before using a piece of borrowed information.

Even facts that are true and have a sharp impact on the argument may not be relevant to the case at hand.

1. Health statistics from an entire state may have no relevance, or little relevance, to a particular county or zip code. Statistics from an entire country cannot be used to prove very much about a particular state or county.
2. An analogy can be useful in making a point, but the comparison must match up in all characteristics, or it will not be relevant. Analogy should be used very carefully. It is often as likely to destroy an argument as it is to strengthen it.

The importance or significance of a fact may not be sufficient to strengthen an argument. For example, of the millions of immigrants in the U.S., using a single family to support a solution to the immigration problem will not make much difference overall even though those single-example arguments are often used to support one approach or another. They may achieve a positive reaction, but they will not prove that one solution is better than another. If enough cases were cited from a variety of geographical locations, the information might be significant.

How much is enough? Generally speaking, three strong supporting facts are sufficient to establish the thesis of an argument. For example:

Conclusion: All green apples are sour.

- When I was a child, I bit into a green apple from my grandfather's orchard, and it was sour.
- I once bought green apples from a roadside vendor, and, when I bit into one, it was sour.
- My grocery store had a sale on green Granny Smith apples last week, and I bought several only to find that they were sour when I bit into one.

The fallacy in the above argument is that the sample was insufficient. A more exhaustive search would probably turn up some green apples that were not sour.

Sometimes, more than three arguments is too many. On the other hand, it's not unusual to hear public speakers, particularly politicians, who will cite a long litany of facts to support their positions.

A very good example of the effect of omitting facts in an argument is this résumé situation. An applicant is arguing that he or she should be chosen for a particular job. The application form asks for information about past employment, and unfavorable dismissals from jobs in the past may just be omitted. Employers are usually suspicious of periods of time when an applicant has not listed an employer.

A writer makes choices about which facts will be used and which will be discarded in developing an argument. Those choices may exclude anything that is not supportive of the point of view the writer is taking. It's always a good idea for readers to do some research in order to spot these omissions and to ask whether they have an impact on acceptance of the point of view presented in the argument. No judgment is either black or white. If the argument seems too neat or too compelling, there are probably facts that might be relevant that have not been included.

Skill 1.7   Recognize the various persuasive techniques used by an author in a reading selection

Persuasive writing features facts and opinions that are used to get readers to agree with something that the author believes. Persuasive writing may have as its purpose getting you to change your mind, take a position on an issue, perform an action, or judge an event. Of course, there are many different ways to accomplish these goals. Authors may be straightforward and objective, in which case they will marshal a number of facts in support of a position. Alternatively, authors may use emotional words and, in so doing, reveal their personal preferences, biases, or strongly held opinions. While news stories seek to inform, other commonly read material such as editorials, reviews, and letters generally contain an element of persuasion.

Sample Passage and Analysis

Recent scientific research indicates that individuals who wish to lead long, healthy lives should switch from a meat-based to a vegetarian diet. The medical basis for this switch is irrefutable. One clinical study, published in Cancer Research, found that meat-eaters are twice as likely to die from cancer as vegetarians. Moreover, changing to a low-fat, high-fiber vegetarian lifestyle incorporating healthy exercise and stress reduction techniques has been shown to reverse hardening of the arteries and to lower blood pressure in patients suffering from heart disease. Other medical benefits may include the prevention of diabetes, gallstones, and osteoporosis and reductions in the severity and frequency of asthma attacks.

Though the paragraph uses unemotional words and facts to support the position that vegetarianism is preferable to a meat-based diet, close reading reveals why the writer's purpose is to persuade. First, the statement "The medical basis for this switch is irrefutable" indicates an absolute commitment to a position and to the belief that you ought to agree with that position. But while one clinical study is solid support for the author's belief, it is hardly irrefutable. Second, though the author doesn't specifically tell you to change to a vegetarian diet, the first sentence makes it clear that he or she thinks you should do so. In fact, that sentence contains the main idea, which is supported with persuasive reasoning and supporting details. Because the author implicitly invites you to change behavior, this paragraph is classified as persuasive.

Skill 1.8   Distinguish between facts and opinions in a reading selection

Facts are statements that are verifiable. Opinions are statements that must be supported in order to be accepted, such as beliefs, values, judgments, or feelings. Facts are objective information used to support subjective opinions. For example, "Jane is a bad girl" is an opinion. However, "Jane hit her sister with a baseball bat" is a *fact* upon which the opinion is based. Judgments are opinions—decisions or declarations based on observation or reasoning that express approval or disapproval. Facts report what has happened or exists and come from observation, measurement, or calculation. Facts can be tested and verified, whereas opinions and judgments cannot. They can only be supported with facts.

Most statements cannot be so clearly distinguished. "I believe that Jane is a bad girl" is a fact. The speaker knows what he or she believes. However, it obviously includes a judgment that could be disputed by another person who might believe otherwise. Judgments are not usually so firm. They are, rather, plausible opinions that provoke thought or lead to factual development.

Joe DiMaggio, a Yankees center fielder, was replaced by Mickey Mantle in 1952.

This is a fact. If necessary, evidence can be produced to support this.

First year players are more ambitious than seasoned players.
This is an opinion. There is no proof to support that this is true in every case.

Practice Questions: Decide if the statement is fact or opinion.

1. The Inca were a group of Indians who ruled an empire in South America.

   (A) fact
   (B) opinion

2. The Inca were clever.

   (A) fact
   (B) opinion

Answers:

1. (A) is the correct answer. Research can prove this to be true.
2. (B) is the correct answer. It is doubtful that all people who have studied the Inca agree with this statement. Therefore, the proof is not conclusive.

Skill 1.9 **Challenge the statements and opinions presented in a reading selection**

Bias is defined as an opinion, feeling, or influence that strongly favors one side in an argument. A statement or passage is biased if an author attempts to convince a reader of something.

Is there evidence of bias in the following statement?

> *Using a calculator cannot help a student understand the process of graphing, so it is a waste of time.*

Since the author makes it perfectly clear that he does not favor the use of the calculator in graphing problems, the answer is yes, there is evidence of bias. He has included his opinion in this statement.

"The sky is blue" expresses a perceptual fact, and "the sky looks like rain" expresses an opinion. This is because one is **readily provable by objective empirical data**, while the other is a **subjective evaluation based upon personal bias**. This means that facts are things that can be proved by widely accepted means of study and experimentation. We can look and see the color of the sky. Since the shade we are observing is expressed as the color blue and is an accepted norm, the observation that the sky is blue is a fact. (Of course, this fact depends on other external factors such as time of day and weather conditions.)

This brings us to our next idea: It looks like rain. This is a subjective observation in that one individual's perception will differ from another. What looks like rain to one person will not necessarily look like rain to another person. The question remains how to differentiate fact from opinion. The best and only way is to ask oneself if what is being stated can be proved from other sources, by other methods, or by the simple process of reasoning.

Primary and secondary sources

The resources used to support a piece of writing can be divided into two major groups: primary sources and secondary sources.

Primary sources are works and records that were created during the period being studied or immediately after it. Secondary sources are works written significantly after the period being studied and are based upon primary sources. Primary sources are the basic materials that provide raw data and information. Secondary sources are the works that contain the explications of, and judgments on, this primary material.

Primary sources include the following kinds of materials:

- Documents that reflect the immediate, everyday concerns of people: memoranda, bills, deeds, charters, newspaper reports, pamphlets, graffiti, popular writings, journals or diaries, records of decision-making bodies, letters, receipts, snapshots, etc.
- Theoretical writings which reflect care and consideration in composition and an attempt to convince or persuade. The topic will generally be deeper and express more pervasive values than is the case with "immediate" documents. These may include newspaper or magazine editorials, sermons, political speeches, philosophical writings, etc.
- Narrative accounts of events, ideas, trends, etc. written with intentionality by someone who was there or who lived in that time period.
- Statistical data, although statistics may be misleading.
- Literature and nonverbal materials, novels, stories, poetry and essays from the period, as well as coins, archaeological artifacts, and art produced during the period.

Secondary sources include the following kinds of materials:

- Books written on the basis of primary materials about the period of time.
- Books written on the basis of primary materials about persons who played a major role in the events under consideration.
- Books and articles written on the basis of primary materials about the culture, the social norms, the language, and the values of the period.
- Quotations from primary sources.
- Statistical data on the period.
- The conclusions and inferences of other historians.
- Multiple interpretations of the ethos of the time.

Guidelines for the use of secondary sources:

1. Do not rely upon only a single secondary source.
2. Check facts and interpretations against primary sources whenever possible.
3. Do not accept the conclusions of historians uncritically.
4. Place greatest reliance on secondary sources created by the best and most respected scholars.
5. Do not use the inferences of other scholars as if they were facts.
6. Ensure that you recognize any bias that writers bring to their interpretation of history.
7. Understand the primary point of the book as a basis for evaluating the value of the material presented in it to your questions.

Skill 1.10   Identify inconsistencies or differences in points of view within one reading selection or between two or more selections

Point of view can be understood in at least two senses.

In a formal sense, it refers to the person of the narration. In this sense, the general format is that it is first person point of view if the narrator is a character in the selection and third person point of view if the narrator is not a character in the selection. Furthermore, in first person point of view, the narrator uses first person pronouns (such as I, we, and me). The narration can also include third person pronouns (such as he, she, and them), and even second person pronouns (such as you, your, and yours). In third person point of view, the narrator does not use first person pronouns, but can use third and, rarely, second person pronouns. First person point of view establishes a more intimate tone, while third person point of view establishes a more objective tone.

Point of view can be understood in a more general sense to refer to the particular way that a stakeholder in a given situation sees or presents information. Thus, any situation can be presented from various points of view.

Authors sometimes intentionally manipulate the formal point of view for various purposes, and they also often employ different points of view in the general sense to add resonance, thoroughness, fairness, and/or complexity to their material. As an initial step in trying to understand an author's intent, readers can keep track of the dynamics of point of view present in the target text(s).

Keeping track of point of view in either the formal and/or the general sense(s) or both is clearly an important skill to apply to any text. For instance, if a particular character in a story has a major change of circumstances, his or her point of view on many topics may shift, and the author expects readers to notice the shifts. Otherwise, the story disintegrates. Additionally, if an author switches from first person to third person narration, readers are expected to address what the purpose of such a switch might be.

As an example of the importance of being able to identify differences in points of view in a reading selection, consider Shirley Jackson's short story, "Charles." Jackson presents the story through a first person narrator, a mother describing her son's experiences in kindergarten. The mother describes how her once polite son, Laurie, began to exhibit troublesome behaviors at home and how he spoke daily about the misbehavior of a wild child, Charles, at kindergarten. The mother assumes that the bad influence of Charles is rubbing off on Laurie. As the story progresses, Jackson plants a few point of view clues that lead careful readers to begin to question Laurie's credibility. At the end of the story, readers learn along with the narrator that there is no Charles in Laurie's class, the assumption being that Laurie had invented Charles to cover his own misbehavior. The mother's point of view, clearly, undergoes a change.

Skill 1.11   Recognize the audience that a reading selection addresses

Tailoring language for a particular **audience** is an important competency. Writing to be read by a business associate will surely sound different from writing to be read by a younger sibling. Not only will the vocabularies be different, but the formality of the discourse will also need to be adjusted.

The things to be aware of in determining what the language should be for a particular audience, then, hinges on two things: **word choice** and **formality**. The most formal language does not use contractions or slang. The most informal language will probably feature a more casual use of common sayings and anecdotes. Formal language will use longer sentences and will not sound like conversation. The most informal language will use shorter sentences—not necessarily simple sentences—but shorter constructions and may sound like conversation.

In both formal and informal writing, there exists a **tone**, the writer's attitude toward the material and/or readers. Tone may be playful, formal, intimate, angry, serious, ironic, outraged, baffled, tender, serene, depressed, etc. The overall tone of a piece of writing is dictated by both the subject matter and the audience. Tone is also related to the actual words that make up the document, because we attach affective meanings called **connotations** to words. Gaining this conscious control over language makes it possible to use language appropriately in various situations and to evaluate its uses in literature and other forms of communication. By evoking the proper responses from readers/listeners, we can prompt them to take action.

Considering the following questions is an excellent way to assess the audience and tone of a given piece of writing.

1. Who is your audience? (friend, teacher, business person, someone else)
2. How much does this person know about you and/or your topic?
3. What is your purpose? (to prove an argument, to persuade, to amuse, to register a complaint, to ask for a raise, etc.)
4. What emotions do you have about the topic? (nervous, happy, confident, angry, sad, no feelings at all)
5. What emotions do you want to register with your audience? (anger, nervousness, happiness, boredom, interest)
6. What persona do you need to create in order to achieve your purpose?
7. What choice of language is best suited to achieving your purpose with your particular subject? (slang, friendly but respectful, formal)
8. What emotional quality do you want to transmit to achieve your purpose (matter of fact, informative, authoritative, inquisitive, sympathetic, angry) and to what degree do you want to express this tone?

Skill 1.12   **Given the intended audience and purpose, recognize language that creates an inappropriate or inconsistent tone**

o   See Skill 1.11

COMPETENCY 2.0   COMPREHENSION AND CONTEXT

Skill 2.1   Identify the relationships between general and specific ideas in a reading selection

From general to specific is a continuum. In other words, a term or phrase may be more specific than another term or more general than another one. For example, car is about the middle of a continuum; however, if I mention John Smith's car, it has become more specific. The most specific is a unique item: John Smith's 2007 Lexus, serial #000000000. *Cars* is a general term that can be narrowed and narrowed and narrowed to suit whatever purposes the writer has for the term. For instance, it would be possible to make a statement about all the cars in the United States, which has been narrowed somewhat from cars. It is, however, still a very general term. A thesis statement is typically a generality: All the cars in the United States run on gasoline. Then specifics would be needed to support that generalization.

Skill 2.2   Determine the sequence of events or steps in a process from a reading selection

The ability to organize events or steps presented in a passage (especially when presented in random order) encourages the development of logical thinking, analysis, and evaluation.

Working through and discussing with your students examples like the one below gives the students valuable practice in sequencing events.

Practice Question: Identify the proper order of events or steps.

1. Matt tied a knot in his shoelace.
2. Matt put on his green socks because they were clean and complemented the brown slacks he was wearing.
3. Matt took a bath and trimmed his toenails.
4. Matt put on his brown slacks.

Answer: The proper order of events is: 3, 4, 2, 1.

Skill 2.3   Arrange the ideas in a reading selection into an outline or other form of graphic organization

Sample Passage

Chili peppers may turn out to be the wonder drug of the decade. The fiery fruit comes in many sizes, shapes, and colors, all of which grow on plants that are genetic descendants of the tepin plant, originally native to the Americas. Connoisseurs of the regional cuisines of the Southwest and Louisiana are already well aware that food flavored with chilies can cause a good sweat, but medical researchers are learning more every day about the medicinal power of capsaicin, the ingredient in the peppers that produces the heat.

Capsaicin as a pain medication has been a part of folk medicine for centuries. It is, in fact, the active ingredient in several currently available, over-the-counter liniments for sore muscles. Recent research has been examining the value of the compound for the treatment of other painful conditions. Capsaicin shows some promise in the treatment of phantom-limb syndrome, shingles, and some types of headaches. Additional research focuses upon the use of capsaicin to relieve pain in post-surgical patients. Scientists speculate that application of the compound to the skin causes the body to release endorphins – natural pain relievers manufactured by the body itself. An alternative theory holds that capsaicin somehow interferes with the transmission of signals along nerve fibers, thus reducing the sensation of pain.

In addition to its well-documented history as a pain killer, capsaicin has recently received attention as a phytochemical, one of the naturally occurring compounds from foods that show cancer-fighting qualities. Like the phytochemical sulfoaphane found in broccoli, capsaicin might turn out to be an agent capable of short-circuiting the actions of carcinogens at the cell level before they can cause cancer.

Summary: Chili peppers contain a chemical called capsaicin which has proved useful for treating a variety of ailments. Recent research reveals that capsaicin is a phytochemical, a natural compound that may help fight cancer.

Outline: -Chili peppers could be the wonder drug of the decade
-Chili peppers contain capsaicin
-Capsaicin can be used as a pain medication
-Capsaicin is a phytochemical
-Phytochemicals show cancer-fighting qualities
-Capsaicin might be able to short-circuit the effects of carcinogens

Skill 2.4   Recognize the main idea or purpose of a reading selection

The main idea of a passage or paragraph is the basic message, idea, point concept, or meaning that the author wants to convey to you, the reader. Understanding the main idea of a passage or paragraph is the key to understanding the more subtle components of the author's message. The main idea is what is being said about a topic or subject. Once you have identified the basic message, you will have an easier time answering other questions that test critical skills.

Main ideas are either *stated* or *implied*. A *stated main idea* is explicit: It is directly expressed in a sentence or two in the paragraph or passage. An *implied main idea* is suggested by the overall reading selection. In the first case, you need not pull information from various points in the paragraph or passage in order to determine the main idea because it is already stated by the author. If a main idea is implied, however, you must formulate it in your own words by condensing the overall message expressed through the passage.

Practice Question: Read the following passage and select an answer.

Sometimes too much of a good thing can become a very bad thing indeed. In an earnest attempt to consume a healthy diet, dietary-supplement enthusiasts have been known to overdose. Vitamin C, for example, long thought to help people ward off cold viruses, is currently being studied for its possible role in warding off cancer and other diseases that cases tissue degeneration. Unfortunately, an overdose of vitamin C – more than 10,000 mg – on a daily basis can cause nausea and diarrhea. Calcium supplements, commonly taken by women, are helpful in warding off osteoporosis. More than just a few grams a day, however, can lead to stomach upset and even to kidney and bladder stones. Niacin, proven useful in reducing cholesterol levels, can be dangerous in large doses to those who suffer from heart problems, asthma, or ulcers.

The main idea expressed in this paragraph is:

  A. Supplements taken in excess can be a bad thing.
  B. Dietary supplement enthusiasts have been known to overdose.
  C. Vitamins can cause nausea, diarrhea, and kidney or bladder stones.
  D. People who take supplements are preoccupied with their health.

Answer: Answer A is a paraphrase of the first sentence and provides a general framework for the rest of the paragraph: Excess supplement intake is bad. The rest of the paragraph discusses the consequences of taking too many vitamins. Options B and C refer to major details, and Option D introduces the idea of preoccupation, which is not included in this paragraph.

Skill 2.5 Identify accurate paraphrases or summaries of ideas in a reading selection

o See Skill 2.3

Skill 2.6 Identify facts and details presented in a reading selection

o See Skill 1.2

Skill 2.7 Draw conclusions or generalizations from material presented in a reading selection

In developing a line of reasoning, writers choose either inductive, going from the specific to the general, or deductive, going from the general to the specific. Inductive reasoning is suggested by the following sentences: "I tasted a green apple from my grandfather's yard when I was five years old, and it was sour. I also tasted a green apple that my friend brought to school in his lunchbox when I was eight years old, and it was sour. I was in Browns Roadside Market and bought some green Granny Smith apples last week, and they were sour." This is a series of specifics. From those specifics, I might draw a conclusion—a generalization—all green apples are sour, and I would have reasoned inductively to arrive at that generalization.

The same simplistic argument developed deductively would begin with the generalization that all green apples are sour. Then specifics would be offered to support that generalization: the sour green apple I tasted in my grandfather's orchard, the sour green apple in my friend's lunchbox, and the Granny Smith apples from the market.

When reasoning is this simple and straightforward, it's easy to follow, but it's also easy to see fallacies. For example, this person hasn't tasted all the green apples in the world; and, in fact, some green apples are not sour. However, it's rarely that easy to see the generalizations and the specifics. In determining whether a point has been proven, it's necessary to do that.

Sometimes generalizations are cited on the assumption that they are commonly accepted and do not need to be supported. An example: All men die sooner or later. Examples wouldn't be needed because that is commonly accepted. Now, some people might require that "die" be defined, but even the definition of "die" is assumed in this generalization.

Here are some current generalizations that may command common acceptance: Providing healthcare for all citizens is the responsibility of the government; All true patriots will support any war the government declares.

Skill 2.8   Make inferences and recognize implications based on information from a reading selection

    o   See Skill 1.3

Skill 2.9   Recognize implied relationships between people, ideas, or events in a reading selection

Good writing features relationships between sentences that conceptually tie one sentence to another. The relationships may be explicit, in which case a transition or clue word helps to identify the connection. The relationships may be implicit, in which case you must closely examine the elements found in each sentence to infer the relationships.

Most sentences cannot meaningfully stand alone. To read a passage without recognizing how each sentence is linked to those around it is to lose the passage's meaning. There are many ways in which sentences can be connected to one another:

Addition – one sentence is "tacked on" to another without making one sentence depend upon the other. Both are equally important.

> *Joanna recently purchased a new stereo system, computer, and home alarm system. She **also** put a downpayment on a new automobile.*

Clarification – One sentence restates the point of an earlier one, but in different terms.

> *The national debt is growing continually. **In fact**, by next year it may be five trillion dollars.*

Comparison/Contrast – Connection is one of similarity or difference.

> *Shelley's strained relationship with his father led the poet to a life of rebellion. **Likewise**, Byron's Bohemian lifestyle may be traced to his ambivalence towards authority.*

Example – One sentence works to make another more concrete or specific.

> *Sarah has always been an optimistic person. She believes that when she graduates from college she will get the job of her choice. (implicit)*

Location/Spatial Order – The relationship between sentences shows the placement of objects or items relative to each other in space.

> *The park was darkened by the school building's shadow. However, the sun still splashed the front window with light. (implicit)*

Cause/Effect – One event (cause) brings about the second event (effect).

> *General Hooker failed to anticipate General Lee's bold maneuver.* **As a result**, *Hooker's army was nearly routed by a smaller force. (explicit)*

Summary – A summary sentence surveys and captures the most important points of the previous sentence(s).

> *Every Fourth of July Ralph brings his whole family to the local parade, every Memorial Day he displays the flag, and every November fourth he votes.* **On the whole**, *he's a patriotic American. (explicit)*

Skill 2.10	Use context clues, syntax, and structural analysis (e.g., affixes, prefixes, roots) to determine the meaning of unknown words

Context clues help readers determine the meaning of words they are not familiar with. The context of a word is the sentence or sentences that surround the word.

Read the following sentences and attempt to determine the meanings of the words in bold print.

> The **luminosity** of the room was so incredible that there was no need for lights.

>> If there was no need for lights then one must assume that the word luminosity has something to do with giving off light. The definition of luminosity is the emission of light.

> Jamie could not understand Joe's feelings. His mood swings made understanding him somewhat of an **enigma.**

>> The fact that he could not be understood made him somewhat of a puzzle. The definition of enigma is a mystery or puzzle.

Familiarity with word roots (the basic elements of words) and with prefixes can also help one determine the meanings of unknown words.

Following is a partial list of roots and prefixes. It might be useful to review these.

Root	Meaning	Example
aqua	water	aqualung
astro	stars	astrology
bio	life	biology
carn	meat	carnivorous
circum	around	circumnavigate
geo	earth	geology
herb	plant	herbivorous
mal	bad	malicious
neo	new	neonatal
tele	distant	telescope

Prefix	Meaning	Example
un-	not	unnamed
re-	again	reenter
il-	not	illegible
pre-	before	preset
mis-	incorrectly	misstate
in-	not	informal
anti-	against	antiwar
de-	opposite	derail
post-	after	postwar
ir-	not	irresponsible

Reading in your spare time - newspapers, magazines, novels - can also help to increase your overall vocabulary.

Word forms

Sometimes a very familiar word can appear as a different part of speech.

You may have heard that *fraud* involves a criminal misrepresentation, so when it appears as the adjective form *fraudulent* ("He was suspected of fraudulent activities"), you can make an educated guess.

You probably know that something out of date is *obsolete;* therefore, when you read about "built-in *obsolescence,*" you can detect the meaning of the unfamiliar word.

Practice Questions: Read the following sentences and attempt to determine the meaning of the underlined words.

1. Farmer John got a two-horse plow and went to work. Straight <u>furrows</u> stretched out behind him.

   The word <u>furrows</u> means

   (A) long cuts made by plow
   (B) vast, open fields
   (C) rows of corn
   (D) pairs of hitched horses

2. The survivors struggled ahead, <u>shambling</u> through the terrible cold, doing their best not to fall.

   The word <u>shambling</u> means

   (A) frozen in place
   (B) running
   (C) shivering uncontrollably
   (D) walking awkwardly

Answers:

1. (A) is the correct answer. The words "straight" and the expression "stretched out behind him" are your clues.

2. (D) is the correct answer. The words "struggled" and "doing their best not to fall" are your clues.

The context for a word is the written passage that surrounds it. Sometimes the writer offers synonyms—words that have nearly the same meaning. Context clues can appear within the sentence itself, within the preceding and/or following sentence(s), or in the passage as a whole.

Sentence clues

Often, a writer will actually **define** a difficult or particularly important word for you the first time it appears in a passage. Phrases like *that is, such as, which is,* or *is called* might announce the writer's intention to give just the definition you need. Occasionally, a writer will simply use a synonym (a word that means the same thing) or near-synonym joined by the word *or*. Look at the following examples:

> The <u>credibility,</u> that is to say the believability, of the witness was called into question by evidence of previous perjury.
> Nothing would <u>assuage</u> or lessen the child's grief.

Punctuation at the sentence level is often a clue to the meaning of a word. Commas, parentheses, quotation marks, and dashes tell the reader that a definition is being offered by the writer.

> A tendency toward <u>hyperbole,</u> extravagant exaggeration, is a common flaw among persuasive writers.

> Political <u>apathy</u> - lack of interest - can lead to the death of the state.

A writer might simply give an **explanation** in other words that you can understand, in the same sentence:

> The <u>xenophobic</u> townspeople were suspicious of every foreigner.

Writers also explain a word in terms of its opposite at the sentence level:

> His <u>incarceration</u> was ended, and he was elated to be free.

Skill 2.11 Determine the meanings of figurative or colloquial language in a reading selection

Figurative Language: Not meant in a literal sense, but meant to be interpreted as symbolic. Figurative language is made up of such literary devices as hyperbole, metonymy, synecdoche, and oxymoron. A synecdoche is a figure of speech in which the word for part of something is used to mean the whole; for example, "sail" for "boat," or vice versa.

1. Simile: Indirect comparison between two things. "My love is like a red-red rose."
2. Metaphor: Direct comparison between two things. The use of a word or phrase denoting one kind of object or action in place of another to suggest a comparison between them. While poets use them extensively, they are also integral to everyday speech. For example, a tenacious person might be called a bulldog.
3. Parallelism: The arrangement of ideas in phrases, sentences, and paragraphs that balance one element with another of equal importance and similar wording. An example from Francis Bacon's *Of Studies:* "Reading maketh a full man, conference a ready man, and writing an exact man."
4. Personification: Human characteristics are attributed to an inanimate object, an abstract quality, or animal. Examples: John Bunyan created characters named Death, Knowledge, Giant Despair, Sloth, and Piety in his *Pilgrim's Progress.* The metaphor of an arm of a chair is a form of personification.
5. Euphemism: The substitution of an agreeable or inoffensive term for one that might offend or suggest something unpleasant. Many euphemisms are used to refer to death in order to avoid using the real word, such as "passed away," "crossed over," or, nowadays, "passed."
6. Hyperbole: Deliberate exaggeration for effect or comic effect. An example from Shakespeare's *The Merchant of Venice*:
   > Why, if two gods should play some heavenly match
   > And on the wager lay two earthly women,
   > And Portia one, there must be something else
   > Pawned with the other, for the poor rude world
   > Hath not her fellow.
7. Climax: A number of phrases or sentences are arranged in ascending order of rhetorical forcefulness. Example from Melville's *Moby Dick*:
   All that most maddens and torments; all that stirs up the lees of things; all truth with malice in it; all that cracks the sinews and cakes the brain; all the subtle demonisms of life and thought; all evil, to crazy Ahab, were visibly personified and made practically assailable in Moby Dick.
8. Bathos: A ludicrous attempt to portray pathos—that is, to evoke pity, sympathy, or sorrow. It may result from inappropriately dignifying the commonplace, elevated language to describe something trivial, or greatly exaggerated pathos.

9. Oxymoron: A contradiction in terms deliberately employed for effect. It is usually seen in a qualifying adjective whose meaning is contrary to that of the noun it modifies, such as wise folly.

10. Irony: Intending to convey something other than and practically opposite of the literal meaning, such as words of praise when blame is intended. In poetry, it is often used as a sophisticated or resigned awareness of contrast between what is and what ought to be and expresses a controlled pathos without sentimentality. It is a form of indirection that avoids overt praise or censure. An early example: the Greek comic character Eiron, a clever underdog who by his wit repeatedly triumphs over the boastful character Alazon.

11. Alliteration: The repetition of consonant sounds in two or more neighboring words or syllables. In its simplest form, it reinforces one or two consonant sounds. Example: Shakespeare's Sonnet #12:

    When I do count the clock that tells the time.

    Some poets have used more complex patterns of alliteration by creating consonants both at the beginning of words and at the beginning of stressed syllables within words. Example: Shelley's "Stanzas Written in Dejection Near Naples":

    The City's voice itself is soft like Solitude's

12. Onomatopoeia: The naming of a thing or action by a vocal imitation of the sound associated with it, such as *buzz* or *hiss* or the use of words whose sound suggests the meaning. Example from "The Brook" by Tennyson:

    I chatter over stony ways,
    In little sharps and trebles,
    I bubble into eddying bays,
    I babble on the pebbles.

Skill 2.12   Recognize and identify different interpretations that can be made of the same word, sentence, paragraph, or reading selection

Informative denotations

Informative denotations are definitions agreed upon by the society in which the learner operates. A *skunk* is "a black and white mammal of the weasel family with a pair of perineal glands which secrete a pungent odor." The *Merriam Webster Collegiate Dictionary* adds "...and offensive" odor. Identification of the color, species, and glandular characteristics are informative. The interpretation of the odor as *offensive* is affective.

Affective connotations

Affective connotations are the personal feelings a word arouses. A child who has no personal experience with a skunk and its odor or has had a pet skunk will feel differently about the word *skunk* than a child who has smelled the spray or been conditioned vicariously to associate offensiveness with the animal denoted by *skunk*. The very fact that our society views a skunk as an animal to be avoided will affect children's interpretation of the word. In fact, it is not necessary for one to have actually seen a skunk (that is, have a denotative understanding) to use the word in a connotative expression. For example, children might call each other skunks, connoting an unpleasant reaction (affective use). Still, they would be able to use the same word to refer to the small black and white animal.

Using connotations

In everyday language, we attach affective meanings to words unconsciously; we exercise more conscious control of informative denotations. In the process of language development, the learner must come not only to grasp the definitions of words, but also to grasp their affective connotations and how people process these connotations. Gaining this conscious control over language makes it possible to use language appropriately in various situations and to evaluate its uses in literature and other forms of communication.

The manipulation of language for a variety of purposes is the goal of language instruction. Advertisers and satirists are especially conscious of the effect word choice has on their audiences. By evoking the proper responses from readers and listeners, we can prompt them to take action.

Skill 2.13   Recognize how the meaning of a word, sentence, or paragraph is affected by the context in which it appears

o   See Skill 2.11

Skill 2.14   Understand the function of key transition indicators in a reading selection (e.g., "however," "by contrast," "in conclusion")

Transitions, words that signal relationships between ideas, can help improve the flow of a document. Transitions can help achieve a clear and effective presentation of information by establishing connections between sentences, paragraphs, and sections of a document. With transitions, each sentence builds on the ideas in the last, and each paragraph has clear links to the preceding ones. As a result, readers receive clear directions on how to piece together writers' ideas to form a logically coherent argument. By signaling how to organize, interpret, and react to information, transitions allow writers to effectively and elegantly explain their ideas.

Logical Relationship	Transitional Expression
Similarity	also, in the same way, just as ... so too, likewise, similarly
Exception/Contrast	but, however, in spite of, on the one hand ... on the other hand, nevertheless, nonetheless, notwithstanding, in contrast, on the contrary, still, yet
Sequence/Order	first, second, third, ... next, then, finally
Time	after, afterward, at last, before, currently, during, earlier, immediately, later, meanwhile, now, recently, simultaneously, subsequently, then
Example	for example, for instance, namely, specifically, to illustrate
Emphasis	even, indeed, in fact, of course, truly
Place/Position	above, adjacent, below, beyond, here, in front, in back, nearby, there
Cause and Effect	accordingly, consequently, hence, so, therefore, thus
Additional Support or Evidence	additionally, again, also, and, as well, besides, equally important, further, furthermore, in addition, moreover, then
Conclusion/Summary	finally, in a word, in brief, in conclusion, in the end, in the final analysis, on the whole, thus, to conclude, to summarize, in sum, in summary

The following example shows good logical order and transitions

No one really knows how Valentine's Day started. There are several legends, however, which are often told. The first attributes Valentine's Day to a Christian priest who lived in Rome during the third century under the rule of Emperor Claudius. Rome was at war, and apparently Claudius felt that married men didn't fight as well as bachelors. Consequently, Claudius banned marriage for the duration of the war. But Valentinus, in violation of Claudius' law, risked his life to secretly marry couples. The second legend is even more romantic. In this story, Valentinus is a prisoner condemned to death for refusing to worship pagan deities. While in jail, he fell in love with his jailer's daughter, who happened to be blind. Daily, he prayed for her sight to return and, miraculously, it did. On February 14, the day that he was scheduled to die, he was allowed to write the young woman a note. In this farewell letter, he promised eternal love and signed at the bottom of the page the now famous words, "Your Valentine."

COMPETENCY 3.0   RESEARCH AND REFERENCE

Skill 3.1   Use the table of contents, section headings, index, and other sections of a book to locate information

In nonfiction text, it is important to use the specific features of these types of texts to help locate information in a rapid and fluid manner.

When looking at a table of contents, it is important to keep in mind that the chapter titles are broad, and that many narrow topics can fall under those broader topics. This allows you to narrow down where to search within the text and to save time. Think of the chapter title listed on the table of contents as a one sentence or less summary of the content found in that chapter. If your topic fits under that summary, you know where to start looking. The table of contents includes chapter titles and the pages on which they begin.

Once in the chapter, you can use the section headings to further narrow your search procedure. If you think of the chapter titles listed on the table of contents as a summary, think of the section headings as bullets listing the subtitles. Section headings provide you with an even narrower focus of where to locate specific information. They are smaller units and more specific than the information found in the table of contents. Section headings are usually bolded and are found within the text.

If you have a very specific topic, you may want to start with the index. The index lists specific topics alphabetically. It will be the most detailed, providing you with a page number for the information. It is the fastest and easiest way to find the page on which information is located.

The table of contents, the section headings, and the index are tools to help you locate information within text quickly and efficiently. They can be thought of as similar to an outline for the reading.

Skill 3.2   Locate the place in a reading selection (e.g., book, chapter, paragraph, article, or report) where a specific kind of information can be found

o   *See Skill 3.1*

Skill 3.3   Understand how a reading selection is organized

The **organization** of a written work pertains to the order in which the writer has chosen to present the different parts of the discussion or argument and to the relationships he or she constructs among these parts.

Written ideas need to be presented in a **logical order** so that a reader can follow the information easily and quickly. There are many different ways in which to order a series of ideas, but they all share one common goal: to lead the reader along a desired path in order to give a clear, strong presentation of the writer's main idea. These are some of the ways in which a paragraph may be organized:

Sequence of events – In this type of organization, the details are presented in the order in which they have occurred. Paragraphs that describe a process or procedure, give directions, or outline a given period of time (such as a day or a month) are often arranged chronologically.

Statement support – In this type of organization, the main idea is stated, and the rest of the paragraph explains or proves it. This is also referred to as order of relative importance. There are four ways in which this type of order is organized: most-to-least, least-to-most, most-least-most, and least-most-least.

Comparison-Contrast – In this type of organization, the compare-contrast pattern is used when a paragraph describes the differences or similarities of two or more ideas, actions, events, or things. Usually, the topic sentence describes the basic relationship between or among the ideas or items and the rest of the paragraph explains this relationship in more detail.

Classification – in this type of organization, the paragraph presents grouped information about a topic. The topic sentence usually states the general category, and the rest of the sentences show how (and to what extent) various elements of the category have a common base.

Cause and Effect – This pattern describes how two or more events are connected. The main sentence usually states the primary cause(s), the primary effect(s), and how they are basically connected. The rest of the sentences explain the connection in more detail.

Spatial/Place – In this type of organization, certain descriptions are organized according to the location of items in relation to each other and to a larger context. The orderly arrangement guides readers' eyes as they mentally envision the scene or place being described.

Example, Clarification, and Definition – These types of organizations show, explain, or elaborate on the main idea. This can be done by showing specific cases, by examining meaning multiple times, or by describing one item extensively.

Sample Test

Reading

Read the passages and answer the questions that follow.

This writer has often been asked to tutor hospitalized children with cystic fibrosis. While undergoing all the precautionary measures to see these children (i.e. scrubbing thoroughly and donning sterilized protective gear), she has often wondered why their parents subject these children to the pressures of schooling and trying to catch up on what they have missed because of hospitalization, which is a normal part of cystic fibrosis patients' lives. These children undergo so many tortuous treatments a day that it seems cruel to expect them to learn as normal children do, especially with their life expectancies being as short as they are.

1. **Does the author present an argument that is valid or invalid concerning the schooling of children with cystic fibrosis?**
   (Rigorous) (Skill 1.6)

   A. Valid

   B. Invalid

2. **Is there evidence of bias in this paragraph?**
   (Rigorous) (Skill 1.7)

   A. Yes

   B. No

3. **The author states that it is "cruel" to expect children with cystic fibrosis to learn as "normal" children do. Is this a fact or an opinion?**
   (Average Rigor) (Skill 1.8)

   A. Fact

   B. Opinion

4. **What is the author's tone?**
   (Average Rigor) (Skill 2.3)

   A. Sympathetic

   B. Cruel

   C. Disbelieving

   D. Cheerful

5. **What is the main idea of this passage?**
(Average Rigor) (Skill 2.4)

   A. There is a lot of preparation involved in visiting a patient with cystic fibrosis.

   B. Children with cystic fibrosis are incapable of living normal lives.

   C. Certain concessions should be made for children with cystic fibrosis.

   D. Children with cystic fibrosis die young.

6. **Why is the author familiar with the procedures used when visiting a child with cystic fibrosis?**
(Easy) (Skill 2.4)

   A. She has read about it.

   B. She works in a hospital.

   C. She is the parent of one.

   D. She often tutors them.

7. **What is the author's purpose?**
(Rigorous) (Skill 2.4)

   A. To inform

   B. To entertain

   C. To describe

   D. To narrate

8. **What kind of relationship is found within the sentence which starts with "These children undergo..." and ends with "...as short as they are"?**
(Rigorous) (Skill 2.7)

   A. Addition

   B. Explanation

   C. Generalization

   D. Classification

9. **What is meant by the word "precautionary" in the second sentence?**
(Average Rigor) (Skill 2.10)

   A. Careful

   B. Protective

   C. Medical

   D. Sterilizing

10. **What type of organizational pattern is the author using?**
(Rigorous) (Skill 3.3)

   A. Classification

   B. Explanation

   C. Comparison and contrast

   D. Cause and effect

Disciplinary practices have been found to affect diverse areas of child development such as the acquisition of moral values, obedience to authority, and performance at school. Even though the dictionary has a specific definition of the word "discipline," it is still open to interpretation by people of different cultures.

There are four types of disciplinary styles: assertion of power, withdrawal of love, reasoning, and permissiveness. Assertion of power involves the use of force to discourage unwanted behavior. Withdrawal of love involves making the love of a parent conditional on a children's good behavior. Reasoning involves persuading children to behave one way rather than another. Permissiveness involves allowing children to do as they please and face the consequences of their actions.

11. **What does the technique of reasoning involve?** *(Easy) (Skill 1.2)*

   A. Persuading children to behave in a certain way.

   B. Allowing children to do as they please.

   C. Using force to discourage unwanted behavior.

   D. Making love conditional on good behavior.

12. **Name four types of disciplinary styles.** *(Easy) (Skill 1.2)*

   A. Reasoning, power assertion, morality, and permissiveness.

   B. Morality, reasoning, permissiveness, and withdrawal of love.

   C. Withdrawal of love, permissiveness, assertion of power, and reasoning.

   D. Withdrawal of love, morality, reasoning, and power assertion.

13. **Is this passage biased?** *(Rigorous) (Skill 1.7)*

   A. Yes

   B. No

14. **The author states that "assertion of power involves the use of force to discourage unwanted behavior." Is this a fact or an opinion?** *(Average Rigor) (Skill 1.8)*

   A. Fact

   B. Opinion

15. **What is the author's tone?**
(Average Rigor) (Skill 2.3)

   A. Disbelieving

   B. Angry

   C. Informative

   D. Optimistic

16. **What is the main idea of this passage?**
(Average Rigor) (Skill 2.4)

   A. Different people have different ideas of how to discipline children.

   B. Permissiveness is the most widely used disciplinary style.

   C. Most people agree on their definition of discipline.

   D. There are four disciplinary styles.

17. **What is the author's purpose in writing this?**
(Easy) (Skill 2.4)

   A. To describe

   B. To narrate

   C. To entertain

   D. To inform

18. **From reading this passage, we can conclude that**
(Rigorous) (Skill 2.7)

   A. the author is a teacher.

   B. the author has many children.

   C. the author has written a book about discipline.

   D. the author has done research on discipline.

19. **What is the meaning of the word "diverse" in the first sentence?**
(Easy) (Skill 2.10)

   A. Many

   B. Related to children

   C. Disciplinary

   D. Moral

20. **What organizational structure is used in the first sentence of the second paragraph?**
(Average Rigor) (Skill 3.3)

   A. Addition

   B. Explanation

   C. Definition

   D. Simple listing

21. **What is the overall organizational pattern of this passage?**
(Rigorous) (Skill 3.3)

A. Generalization

B. Cause and effect

C. Addition

D. Summary

One of the most difficult problems plaguing American education is the assessment of teachers. No one denies that teachers ought to be answerable for what they do, but what exactly does that mean? The Oxford American Dictionary defines accountability as the obligation to give a reckoning or explanation for one's actions.

Does a student have to learn for teaching to have taken place? Historically, teaching has not been defined in this restrictive manner; the teacher was thought to be responsible for the quantity and quality of material covered and the way in which it was presented. However, some definitions of teaching now imply that students must learn in order for teaching to have taken place.

As a teacher who tries my best to keep current on all the latest teaching strategies, I believe that those teachers who do not even bother to pick up an educational journal every once in a while should be kept under close watch. There are many teachers out there who have been teaching for decades and refuse to change their ways even if research has proven that their methods are outdated and ineffective. There is no place in the profession of teaching for these types of individuals. It is time that the American educational system clean house, for the sake of our children.

22. **The author states that teacher assessment is a problem for**
(Easy) (Skill 1.2)

   A. Elementary schools

   B. Secondary schools

   C. American education

   D. Families

23. **Is this a valid argument?**
(Rigorous) (Skill 1.6)

   A. Yes

   B. No

24. **Is there evidence of bias in this passage?**
(Rigorous) (Skill 1.7)

   A. Yes

   B. No

25. **Teachers who do not keep current on educational trends should be fired. Is this a fact or an opinion?**
(Average Rigor) (Skill 1.8)

   A. Fact

   B. Opinion

26. **The author's tone is one of**
(Average Rigor) (Skill 2.3)

   A. Disbelief

   B. Excitement

   C. Support

   D. Concern

27. **What is the author's purpose in writing this?**
(Average Rigor) (Skill 2.4)

   A. To entertain

   B. To narrate

   C. To describe

   D. To persuade

28. **What is the main idea of the passage?**
(Average Rigor) (Skill 2.4)

   A. Teachers should not be answerable for what they do.

   B. Teachers who do not do their job should be fired.

   C. The author is a good teacher.

   D. Assessment of teachers is a serious problem in society today.

29. **Where does the author get her definition of "accountability?"**
(Easy) (Skill 2.6)

   A. Webster's Dictionary

   B. Encyclopedia Britannica

   C. Oxford Dictionary

   D. World Book Encyclopedia

30. **From the passage, one can infer that**
(Average Rigor) (Skill 2.8)

   A. The author considers herself a good teacher.

   B. Poor teachers will be fired.

   C. Students have to learn for teaching to take place.

   D. The author will be fired.

31. **What is the meaning of the word "reckoning" in the third sentence?**
(Easy) (Skill 2.10)

   A. Thought

   B. Answer

   C. Obligation

   D. Explanation

32. **What is meant by the word "plaguing" in the first sentence?**
(Easy) (Skill 2.10)

   A. Causing problems

   B. Causing illness

   C. Causing anger

   D. Causing failure

33. **What is the organizational pattern of the second paragraph?**
(Rigorous) (Skill 3.3)

   A. Cause and effect

   B. Classification

   C. Addition

   D. Explanation

34. **What is the author's overall organizational pattern?**
(Rigorous) (Skill 3.3)

   A. Classification

   B. Cause and effect

   C. Definition

   D. Comparison and contrast

Mr. Smith gave instructions for the painting to be hung on the wall. And then it leaped forth before his eyes: the little cottages on the river, the white clouds floating over the valley, and the green of the towering mountain ranges which were seen in the distance. The painting was so vivid that it seemed almost real. Mr. Smith was now absolutely certain that the painting had been worth the money.

35. **Is this passage biased?**
     (Rigorous) (Skill 1.7)

     A. Yes

     B. No

36. **What is the main idea of this passage?**
     (Average Rigor) (Skill 2.4)

     A. The painting that Mr. Smith purchased was expensive.

     B. Mr. Smith purchased a painting.

     C. Mr. Smith was pleased with the quality of the painting he had purchased.

     D. The painting depicted cottages and valleys.

37. **The author's purpose is to**
     (Rigorous) (Skill 2.4)

     A. Inform

     B. Entertain

     C. Persuade

     D. Narrate

38. **From the last sentence, one can infer that**
     (Rigorous) (Skill 2.8)

     A. The painting was expensive.

     B. The painting was cheap.

     C. Mr. Smith was considering purchasing the painting.

     D. Mr. Smith thought the painting was too expensive and decided not to purchase it.

39. **What is the meaning of the word "vivid" in the third sentence?**
     (Average Rigor) (Skill 2.10)

     A. Lifelike

     B. Dark

     C. Expensive

     D. Big

40. **What does the author mean by the expression "it leaped forth before his eyes"?** *(Average Rigor) (Skill 2.11)*

A. The painting fell off the wall.

B. The painting appeared so real that it was almost three-dimensional.

C. The painting struck Mr. Smith in the face.

D. Mr. Smith was hallucinating.

Chili peppers may turn out to be the wonder drug of the decade. The fiery fruit comes in many sizes, shapes, and colors, all of which grow on plants that are genetic descendants of the tepin plant, originally native to the Americas. Connoisseurs of the regional cuisines of the South west and Louisiana are already well aware that food flavored with chilies can cause a good sweat, but medical researchers are learning more every day about the medicinal power of capsaicin, the ingredient in the peppers that produces the heat.

Capsaicin as a pain medication has been a part of fold medicine for centuries. It is, in fact, the active ingredient in several currently available, over-the-counter liniments for sore muscles. Recent research has been examining the value of the compound for the treatment of other painful conditions. Capsaicin shows some promise in the treatment of phantom-limb syndrome, shingles, and some types of headaches. Additional research focuses upon the use of capsaicin to relieve pain in post-surgical patients. Scientists speculate that application of the compound to the skin causes the body to release endorphins – natural pain relievers manufactured by the body itself. An alternative theory holds that capsaicin somehow interferes with the transmission of signals along the nerve fibers, thus reducing the sensation of pain.

In addition to its well-documented history as a pain killer, capsaicin has recently received attention as a phytochemical, one of the naturally occurring compounds from foods that show cancer-fighting qualities. Like the phytochemical sulfoaphane found in broccoli, capsaicin might turn out to be an agent capable of short-circuiting the actions of carcinogens at the cell level before they can cause cancer.

41. The statement "Chili peppers may turn out to be the wonder drug of the decade," is a statement of:

(Rigorous) (Skill 1.8)

A. fact.

B. opinion

42. The author's primary purpose is to:
(Average Rigor) (Skill 2.4)

A. entertain the reader with unusual stories about chilies.

B. narrate the story of the discovery of capsaicin.

C. describe the medicinal properties of the tepin plant.

D. inform the reader of the medical research about capsaicin.

43. All of the following medical problems have been treated using capsaicin EXCEPT:

(Average Rigor) (Skill 2.6)

A. cancer.

B. shingles.

C. sore muscles.

D. headache.

44. Choose the word or phrase that best identifies the relationship within the sentence beginning "Scientists speculate…"

(Rigorous) (Skill 3.3)

A. addition

B. definition

C. contrast

D. summary

On January 24, 1993, retired Supreme Court Justice Thurgood Marshall, 84, died of heart failure. The media world-wide marked his passing with eulogies, testimonials, remembrances, and biographies. These usually began, "The first black justice on the Supreme Court," and if this alone were his only accomplishment, it would have earned him a place in history. But his legacy was guaranteed as much by his presence in front of the bench as behind it. Thurgood Marshall, attorney-at-law, was creator of the civil rights legislation that took the movement from the marches in the street to the law of the land.

It is easy to see the significance of events in retrospect, but it is difficult while they are occurring. The high school teacher who made Marshall read the Constitution out loud as a punishment could never have foreseen the irony of the act. Marshall's intimate familiarity with the Constitution enabled him to survive the antagonistic nomination hearings in Congress years later. In college, the biology teacher who clashed with Marshall could not have known that by discouraging a would-be dentist, he was creating a dynamic attorney. And, likewise, college classmates like Langston Hughes, who would become a writer; Cab Calloway, who would entertain millions; and Nnamdi Azikiew, who would become president of Nigeria could not know what they had started when they goaded their friend to join them in a vote for the integration of their college's faculty.

Marshall graduated from Lincoln College in 1930 and went on to graduate from Howard University's law school. After struggling in a private practice, he was hired as an assistant attorney for the NAACP. In Texas, he obtained protection for black jurors. In Maryland, he located a college graduate who had been denied admission into the University of Maryland's all-white law school – as Marshall himself had been denied – and took the university to court. Marshall won the case at the local level even though he had anticipated having to take the case to the Supreme Court.

Eventually, Marshall did argue cases in front of the Supreme Court. Many were on the behalf of the NAACP (for whom Marshall won 29 out of 32 cases); and, later, under President Lyndon Johnson, Marshall argued as Solicitor General. His legal <u>acumen</u> was responsible for the Supreme Court's decision that made segregation of buses illegal, a precedent that paved the way for the successful Montgomery, Alabama boycott led by the Reverend Martin Luther King, Jr. As Solicitor General, Marshall argued the case that resulted in the Miranda rule requiring that suspects be informed of their rights. The most famous case that Marshall argued before the Supreme Court was the landmark "Brown vs. Board of Education," which ended legal segregation in schools.

Outspoken and articulate, Thurgood Marshall's work was essentially behind the scenes when contrasted with other leaders in the Civil Rights Movement. But without his expertise and willingness to face prejudice and fear head-on and in the courtroom, the movement could have died. It took the force of law to enable the drive for equality to gain momentum.

45. **What is the tone of this passage?**
(Average Rigor) (Skill 2.3)

A. ironic

B. reverent

C. ambivalent

D. indignant

46. **According to the passage, Thurgood Marshall graduated from law school at which college or university?**
(Easy) (Skill 2.6)

A. Lincoln College

B. University of Maryland

C. University of Alabama

D. Howard University

47. **The writer of this passage is probably:**
(Rigorous) (Skill 2.8)

A. knowledgeable about legal history.

B. touched or saddened by Marshall's death.

C. respectful of the Constitution.

D. actively interested in politics.

48. **The word acumen most nearly means:**
(Average Rigor) (Skill 2.10)

A. wittiness

B. profession

C. expertise

D. assistant

49. **The primary organizational pattern used in this passage is:**
(Rigorous) (Skill 3.3)

A. cause and effect

B. order of importance

C. summary

D. description

50. **What is the relationship between the sentence beginning "It is easy to see..." and the sentence beginning "And, likewise,...?"**
(Rigorous) (Skill 3.3)

A. clarification

B. cause and effect

C. time order

D. order of importance

Answer Key: Reading

1.	B	26.	D
2.	A	27.	D
3.	B	28.	D
4.	A	29.	C
5.	C	30.	A
6.	D	31.	D
7.	C	32.	A
8.	B	33.	D
9.	B	34.	C
10.	B	35.	B
11.	A	36.	C
12.	C	37.	D
13.	B	38.	A
14.	A	39.	A
15.	C	40.	B
16.	A	41.	B
17.	D	42.	D
18.	D	43.	A
19.	A	44.	A
20.	D	45.	B
21.	C	46.	D
22.	C	47.	A
23.	B	48.	C
24.	A	49.	C
25.	B	50.	A

Rigor Table: Reading

	Easy 20%	Average 40%	Rigorous 40%
Questions (50)	6, 11, 12, 17, 19, 22, 29, 31, 32, 46	3, 4, 5, 9, 14, 15, 16, 20, 25, 26, 27, 28, 30, 36, 39, 40, 42, 43, 45, 48	1, 2, 7, 8, 10, 13, 18, 21, 23, 24, 33, 34, 35, 37, 38, 41, 44, 47, 49, 50
TOTALS	10 (20%)	20 (40%)	20 (40%)

Rationales with Sample Questions: Reading

Read the passages and answer the questions that follow.

This writer has often been asked to tutor hospitalized children with cystic fibrosis. While undergoing all the precautionary measures to see these children (i.e. scrubbing thoroughly and donning sterilized protective gear), she has often wondered why their parents subject these children to the pressures of schooling and trying to catch up on what they have missed because of hospitalization, which is a normal part of cystic fibrosis patients' lives. These children undergo so many tortuous treatments a day that it seems cruel to expect them to learn as normal children do, especially with their life expectancies being as short as they are.

1. **Does the author present an argument that is valid or invalid concerning the schooling of children with cystic fibrosis?** *(Rigorous) (Skill 1.6)*

   A. Valid

   B. Invalid

Answer B: Invalid

Even though to most readers, the writer's argument makes good sense, it is biased and lacks real evidence.

2. **Is there evidence of bias in this paragraph?** *(Rigorous) (Skill 1.7)*

   A. Yes

   B. No

Answer A: Yes

The writer clearly feels sorry for these children and gears her writing in that direction.

3. The author states that it is "cruel" to expect children with cystic fibrosis to learn as "normal" children do. Is this a fact or an opinion?
    (Average Rigor) (Skill 1.8)

    A. Fact

    B. Opinion

Answer B: Opinion

The fact that she states that it "seems" cruel indicates there is no evidence to support this belief.

4. What is the author's tone?
    (Average Rigor) (Skill 2.3)

    A. Sympathetic

    B. Cruel

    C. Disbelieving

    D. Cheerful

Answer A: Sympathetic

The author states that "it seems cruel to expect them to learn as normal children do," thereby indicating that she feels sorry for them.

5.   **What is the main idea of this passage?**
        (Average Rigor) (Skill 2.4)

     A. There is a lot of preparation involved in visiting a patient with cystic fibrosis.

     B. Children with cystic fibrosis are incapable of living normal lives.

     C. Certain concessions should be made for children with cystic fibrosis.

     D. Children with cystic fibrosis die young.

Answer C: Certain concessions should be made for children with cystic fibrosis.

The author states that she wonders "why parents subject these children to the pressures of schooling" and that "it seems cruel to expect them to learn as normal children do." In making these statements she appears to be expressing the belief that these children should not have to do what "normal" children do. They have enough to deal with – their illness itself.

6.   **Why is the author familiar with the procedures used when visiting a child with cystic fibrosis?**
        (Easy) (Skill 2.4)

     A. She has read about it.

     B. She works in a hospital.

     C. She is the parent of one.

     D. She often tutors them.

Answer D: She often tutors them.

The writer states this fact in the opening sentence.

7. **What is the author's purpose?**
   (Rigorous) (Skill 2.4)

   A. To inform

   B. To entertain

   C. To describe

   D. To narrate

Answer C: To describe

The author is simply describing her experience in working with children with cystic fibrosis.

8. **What kind of relationship is found within the sentence which starts with "These children undergo..." and ends with "...as short as they are"?**
   (Rigorous) (Skill 2.7)

   A. Addition

   B. Explanation

   C. Generalization

   D. Classification

Answer B: Explanation

In mentioning that their life expectancies are short, she is explaining by giving one reason why it is cruel to expect them to learn as normal children do.

9. **What is meant by the word "precautionary" in the second sentence?**
   (Average Rigor) (Skill 2.10)

   A. Careful

   B. Protective

   C. Medical

   D. Sterilizing

Answer B: Protective

The writer uses expressions such as "protective gear" and "child's protection" to emphasize this.

10. **What type of organizational pattern is the author using?**
    (Rigorous) (Skill 3.3)

    A. Classification

    B. Explanation

    C. Comparison and contrast

    D. Cause and effect

Answer B: Explanation

The author mentions tutoring children with cystic fibrosis in her opening sentence and goes on to "explain" some of these issues that are involved with her job.

Disciplinary practices have been found to affect diverse areas of child development such as the acquisition of moral values, obedience to authority, and performance at school. Even though the dictionary has a specific definition of the word "discipline," it is still open to interpretation by people of different cultures.

There are four types of disciplinary styles: assertion of power, withdrawal of love, reasoning, and permissiveness. Assertion of power involves the use of force to discourage unwanted behavior. Withdrawal of love involves making the love of a parent conditional on a children's good behavior. Reasoning involves persuading children to behave one way rather than another. Permissiveness involves allowing children to do as they please and face the consequences of their actions.

11. **What does the technique of reasoning involve?**
   (Easy) (Skill 1.2)

   A. Persuading children to behave in a certain way.

   B. Allowing children to do as they please.

   C. Using force to discourage unwanted behavior.

   D. Making love conditional on good behavior.

Answer A: Persuading the child to behave in a certain way.

This fact is directly stated in the second paragraph.

12. **Name four types of disciplinary styles.**
   (Easy) (Skill 1.2)

   A. Reasoning, power assertion, morality, and permissiveness.

   B. Morality, reasoning, permissiveness, and withdrawal of love.

   C. Withdrawal of love, permissiveness, assertion of power, and reasoning.

   D. Withdrawal of love, morality, reasoning, and power assertion.

Answer C: Withdrawal of love, permissiveness, assertion of power, and reasoning.

This is directly stated in the second paragraph.

13. **Is this passage biased?**
    (Rigorous) (Skill 1.7)

    A. Yes

    B. No

Answer B: No

If the reader were so inclined, he or she could research discipline and find this same objective information.

14. **The author states that "assertion of power involves the use of force to discourage unwanted behavior." Is this a fact or an opinion?**
    (Average Rigor) (Skill 1.8)

    A. Fact

    B. Opinion

Answer A: Fact

Assertion of power as a disciplinary style is objectively defined this way.

15. **What is the author's tone?**
    (Average Rigor) (Skill 2.3)

    A. Disbelieving

    B. Angry

    C. Informative

    D. Optimistic

Answer C: Informative

The author presents information about discipline styles without commentary.

16. **What is the main idea of this passage?**
(Average Rigor) (Skill 2.4)

    A. Different people have different ideas of how to discipline children.

    B. Permissiveness is the most widely used disciplinary style.

    C. Most people agree on their definition of discipline.

    D. There are four disciplinary styles.

Answer A: Different people have different ideas of how to discipline children.

Choice C is not true; the opposite is stated in the passage. Choice B could be true, but we have no evidence of this. Choice D is just one of the many facts listed in the passage.

17. **What is the author's purpose in writing this?**
(Easy) (Skill 2.4)

    A. To describe

    B. To narrate

    C. To entertain

    D. To inform

Answer D: To inform

The author is providing the reader with information about disciplinary practices.

18.   **From reading this passage, we can conclude that (Rigorous) (Skill 2.7)**

A. the author is a teacher.

B. the author has many children.

C. the author has written a book about discipline.

D. the author has done research on discipline.

Answer D: The author has done a lot of research on discipline.

Given all the facts mentioned in the passage, this is the only inference one can make.

19.   **What is the meaning of the word "diverse" in the first sentence? (Easy) (Skill 2.10)**

A. Many

B. Related to children

C. Disciplinary

D. Moral

Answer A: Many

If diverse is an unknown word, any of the choices other than "Many" would be redundant in the sentence.

20. **What organizational structure is used in the first sentence of the second paragraph?**
    (Average Rigor) (Skill 3.3)

    A. Addition

    B. Explanation

    C. Definition

    D. Simple listing

Answer D: Simple Listing

The author lists the types of disciplinary styles without definition or explanation.

21. **What is the overall organizational pattern of this passage?**
    (Rigorous) (Skill 3.3)

    A. Generalization

    B. Cause and effect

    C. Addition

    D. Summary

Answer C: Addition

The author has taken a subject, in this case discipline, and developed it point by point.

One of the most difficult problems plaguing American education is the assessment of teachers. No one denies that teachers ought to be answerable for what they do, but what exactly does that mean? The Oxford American Dictionary defines accountability as the obligation to give a reckoning or explanation for one's actions.

Does a student have to learn for teaching to have taken place? Historically, teaching has not been defined in this restrictive manner; the teacher was thought to be responsible for the quantity and quality of material covered and the way in which it was presented. However, some definitions of teaching now imply that students must learn in order for teaching to have taken place.

As a teacher who tries my best to keep current on all the latest teaching strategies, I believe that those teachers who do not even bother to pick up an educational journal every once in a while should be kept under close watch. There are many teachers out there who have been teaching for decades and refuse to change their ways even if research has proven that their methods are outdated and ineffective. There is no place in the profession of teaching for these types of individuals. It is time that the American educational system clean house, for the sake of our children.

22. **The author states that teacher assessment is a problem for**
(Easy) (Skill 1.2)

    A. Elementary schools

    B. Secondary schools

    C. American education

    D. Families

Answer C: American education

This fact is directly stated in the first paragraph.

23. **Is this a valid argument?**
(Rigorous) (Skill 1.6)

    A. Yes

    B. No

Answer B: No

In the third paragraph, the author appears to be resentful of lazy teachers.

24.   **Is there evidence of bias in this passage?**
      (Rigorous) (Skill 1.7)

      A. Yes

      B. No

Answer A: Yes

The entire third paragraph is the author's opinion on the matter.

25.   **Teachers who do not keep current on educational trends should be fired. Is this a fact or an opinion?**
      (Average Rigor) (Skill 1.8)

      A. Fact

      B. Opinion

Answer B: Opinion

There may be those who feel they can be good teachers by using old methods.

26.   **The author's tone is one of**
      (Average Rigor) (Skill 2.3)

      A. Disbelief

      B. Excitement

      C. Support

      D. Concern

Answer D: Concern

The author appears concerned with the future of education.

27. **What is the author's purpose in writing this?**
   (Average Rigor) (Skill 2.4)

   A. To entertain

   B. To narrate

   C. To describe

   D. To persuade

Answer D: To persuade

The author does some describing, but the majority of her statements seemed geared towards convincing the reader that teachers who are lazy or who do not keep current should be fired.

28. **What is the main idea of the passage?**
   (Average Rigor) (Skill 2.4)

   A. Teachers should not be answerable for what they do.

   B. Teachers who do not do their job should be fired.

   C. The author is a good teacher.

   D. Assessment of teachers is a serious problem in society today.

Answer D: Assessment of teachers is a serious problem in society today.

Most of the passage is dedicated to elaborating on why teacher assessment is such a problem.

29. **Where does the author get her definition of "accountability?"**
(Easy) (Skill 2.6)

    A. Webster's Dictionary

    B. Encyclopedia Britannica

    C. Oxford Dictionary

    D. World Book Encyclopedia

Answer C: Oxford Dictionary

This is directly stated in the third sentence of the first paragraph.

30. **From the passage, one can infer that**
(Average Rigor) (Skill 2.8)

    A. The author considers herself a good teacher.

    B. Poor teachers will be fired.

    C. Students have to learn for teaching to take place.

    D. The author will be fired.

Answer A: The author considers herself a good teacher.

The first sentence of the third paragraph alludes to this.

31. **What is the meaning of the word "reckoning" in the third sentence?**
(Easy) (Skill 2.10)

    A. Thought

    B. Answer

    C. Obligation

    D. Explanation

Answer D: Explanation

The meaning of this word is directly stated in the same sentence.

32. **What is meant by the word "plaguing" in the first sentence?**
    (Easy) (Skill 2.10)

    A. Causing problems

    B. Causing illness

    C. Causing anger

    D. Causing failure

Answer A: Causing problems

The first paragraph makes this definition clear.

33. **What is the organizational pattern of the second paragraph?**
    (Rigorous) (Skill 3.3)

    A. Cause and effect

    B. Classification

    C. Addition

    D. Explanation

Answer D: Explanation

The author explains what she meant in the section "what exactly does that mean?" in the first paragraph.

34. **What is the author's overall organizational pattern?**
    (Rigorous) (Skill 3.3)

    A. Classification

    B. Cause and effect

    C. Definition

    D. Comparison and contrast

Answer C: Definition

The author identifies teacher assessment as a problem and spends the rest of the passage defining why it is considered a problem.

> Mr. Smith gave instructions for the painting to be hung on the wall. And then it leaped forth before his eyes: the little cottages on the river, the white clouds floating over the valley, and the green of the towering mountain ranges which were seen in the distance. The painting was so vivid that it seemed almost real. Mr. Smith was now absolutely certain that the painting had been worth the money.

35. **Is this passage biased?**
    (Rigorous) (Skill 1.7)

    A. Yes

    B. No

Answer B: No

The author describes what happened when Mr. Smith had his new painting hung on the wall.

36. **What is the main idea of this passage?**
    (Average Rigor) (Skill 2.4)

    A. The painting that Mr. Smith purchased was expensive.

    B. Mr. Smith purchased a painting.

    C. Mr. Smith was pleased with the quality of the painting he had purchased.

    D. The painting depicted cottages and valleys.

Answer C: Mr. Smith was pleased with the quality of the painting he had purchased.

Every sentence in the paragraph alludes to this fact.

37. **The author's purpose is to**
    (Rigorous) (Skill 2.4)

    A. Inform

    B. Entertain

    C. Persuade

    D. Narrate

Answer D: Narrate

The author is simply narrating or telling the story of Mr. Smith and his painting.

38. **From the last sentence, one can infer that**
     (Rigorous) (Skill 2.8)

     A. The painting was expensive.

     B. The painting was cheap.

     C. Mr. Smith was considering purchasing the painting.

     D. Mr. Smith thought the painting was too expensive and decided
        not to purchase it.

Answer A: The painting was expensive.

Choice B is incorrect because, had the painting been cheap, chances are that
Mr. Smith would not have considered his purchase "worth the money." Choices
C and D are ruled out by the fact that the painting had already been purchased.
The author makes this clear when she says, "...the painting had been worth the
money."

39. **What is the meaning of the word "vivid" in the third sentence?**
     (Average Rigor) (Skill 2.10)

     A. Lifelike

     B. Dark

     C. Expensive

     D. Big

Answer A: Lifelike

This is reinforced by the second half of the same sentence.

40. **What does the author mean by the expression "it leaped forth before his eyes"?**
(Average Rigor) (Skill 2.11)

A. The painting fell off the wall.

B. The painting appeared so real that it was almost three-dimensional.

C. The painting struck Mr. Smith in the face.

D. Mr. Smith was hallucinating.

Answer B: The painting appeared so real it was almost three-dimensional.

This is directly stated in the third sentence.

Chili peppers may turn out to be the wonder drug of the decade. The fiery fruit comes in many sizes, shapes, and colors, all of which grow on plants that are genetic descendants of the tepin plant, originally native to the Americas. Connoisseurs of the regional cuisines of the South west and Louisiana are already well aware that food flavored with chilies can cause a good sweat, but medical researchers are learning more every day about the medicinal power of capsaicin, the ingredient in the peppers that produces the heat.

Capsaicin as a pain medication has been a part of fold medicine for centuries. It is, in fact, the active ingredient in several currently available, over-the-counter liniments for sore muscles. Recent research has been examining the value of the compound for the treatment of other painful conditions. Capsaicin shows some promise in the treatment of phantom-limb syndrome, shingles, and some types of headaches. Additional research focuses upon the use of capsaicin to relieve pain in post-surgical patients. Scientists speculate that application of the compound to the skin causes the body to release endorphins – natural pain relievers manufactured by the body itself. An alternative theory holds that capsaicin somehow interferes with the transmission of signals along the nerve fibers, thus reducing the sensation of pain.

In addition to its well-documented history as a pain killer, capsaicin has recently received attention as a phytochemical, one of the naturally occurring compounds from foods that show cancer-fighting qualities. Like the phytochemical sulfoaphane found in broccoli, capsaicin might turn out to be an agent capable of short-circuiting the actions of carcinogens at the cell level before they can cause cancer.

41. **The statement "Chili peppers may turn out to be the wonder drug of the decade," is a statement of:**

    (Rigorous) (Skill 1.8)

    A. fact.

    B. opinion

Answer B: opinion.

This sentence reflects an author's idea that is not based on fact and cannot be proven. It is an opinion.

42.   **The author's primary purpose is to:**
        (Average Rigor) (Skill 2.4)

        A. entertain the reader with unusual stories about chilies.

        B. narrate the story of the discovery of capsaicin.

        C. describe the medicinal properties of the tepin plant.

        D. inform the reader of the medical research about capsaicin.

Answer D: inform the reader of the medical research about capsaicin.

This purpose is conveyed in the last sentence of paragraph one.

43.   **All of the following medical problems have been treated using capsaicin EXCEPT:**

        (Average Rigor) (Skill 2.6)

        A. cancer.

        B. shingles.

        C. sore muscles.

        D. headache.

Answer A: cancer.

Choice A is the exception. The passage states that capsaicin "might turn out to be" effective in fighting cancer, but actual cancer treatments with the drug are not mentioned.

44. **Choose the word or phrase that best identifies the relationship within the sentence beginning "Scientists speculate..."**

    (Rigorous) (Skill 3.3)

    A. addition

    B. definition

    C. contrast

    D. summary

Answer A: addition

The passage states that this is additional information.

On January 24, 1993, retired Supreme Court Justice Thurgood Marshall, 84, died of heart failure. The media world-wide marked his passing with eulogies, testimonials, remembrances, and biographies. These usually began, "The first black justice on the Supreme Court," and if this alone were his only accomplishment, it would have earned him a place in history. But his legacy was guaranteed as much by his presence in front of the bench as behind it. Thurgood Marshall, attorney-at-law, was creator of the civil rights legislation that took the movement from the marches in the street to the law of the land.

It is easy to see the significance of events in retrospect, but it is difficult while they are occurring. The high school teacher who made Marshall read the Constitution out loud as a punishment could never have foreseen the irony of the act. Marshall's intimate familiarity with the Constitution enabled him to survive the antagonistic nomination hearings in Congress years later. In college, the biology teacher who clashed with Marshall could not have known that by discouraging a would-be dentist, he was creating a dynamic attorney. And, likewise, college classmates like Langston Hughes, who would become a writer; Cab Calloway, who would entertain millions; and Nnamdi Azikiew, who would become president of Nigeria could not know what they had started when they goaded their friend to join them in a vote for the integration of their college's faculty.

Marshall graduated from Lincoln College in 1930 and went on to graduate from Howard University's law school. After struggling in a private practice, he was hired as an assistant attorney for the NAACP. In Texas, he obtained protection for black jurors. In Maryland, he located a college graduate who had been denied admission into the University of Maryland's all-white law school – as Marshall himself had been denied – and took the university to court. Marshall won the case at the local level even though he had anticipated having to take the case to the Supreme Court.

Eventually, Marshall did argue cases in front of the Supreme Court. Many were on the behalf of the NAACP (for whom Marshall won 29 out of 32 cases); and, later, under President Lyndon Johnson, Marshall argued as Solicitor General. His legal acumen was responsible for the Supreme Court's decision that made segregation of buses illegal, a precedent that paved the way for the successful Montgomery, Alabama boycott led by the Reverend Martin Luther King, Jr. As Solicitor General, Marshall argued the case that resulted in the Miranda rule requiring that suspects be informed of their rights. The most famous case that Marshall argued before the Supreme Court was the landmark "Brown vs. Board of Education," which ended legal segregation in schools.

Outspoken and articulate, Thurgood Marshall's work was essentially behind the scenes when contrasted with other leaders in the Civil Rights Movement. But without his expertise and willingness to face prejudice and fear head-on and in the courtroom, the movement could have died. It took the force of law to enable the drive for equality to gain momentum.

45. **What is the tone of this passage?**
    (Average Rigor) (Skill 2.3)

    A. ironic

    B. reverent

    C. ambivalent

    D. indignant

Answer B: reverent.

The author outlines the events that led Thurgood Marshall into becoming a lawyer and Supreme Court Justice with respect and reverence.

46. **According to the passage, Thurgood Marshall graduated from law school at which college or university?**
    (Easy) (Skill 2.6)

    A. Lincoln College

    B. University of Maryland

    C. University of Alabama

    D. Howard University

Answer D: Howard University

This fact is stated in third paragraph.

47. **The writer of this passage is probably:**
    (Rigorous) (Skill 2.8)

    A. knowledgeable about legal history.

    B. touched or saddened by Marshall's death.

    C. respectful of the Constitution.

    D. actively interested in politics.

Answer A: knowledgeable about legal history.

The author clearly traces the effects of Marshall's law practice and court decisions on civil rights in the United States.

48. **The word acumen most nearly means:**
    (Average Rigor) (Skill 2.10)

    A. wittiness

    B. profession

    C. expertise

    D. assistant

Answer C: expertise.

The context of the passage indicates that because of Marshall's legal expertise, the Supreme Court decided that segregation of buses was illegal.

49.   **The primary organizational pattern used in this passage is:**
        (Rigorous) (Skill 3.3)

    A. cause and effect

    B. order of importance

    C. summary

    D. description

Answer C: summary

The passage summarizes Thurgood Marshall's accomplishments.

50.   **What is the relationship between the sentence beginning "It is easy to see" and the sentence beginning "And, likewise"?**
        (Rigorous) (Skill 3.3)

    A. clarification

    B. cause and effect

    C. time order

    D. order of importance

Answer A: clarification

The second sentence further clarifies the specific events that led Marshall into law and ultimate influenced civil rights in America.

SUBAREA II.   **MATHEMATICS**

COMPETENCY 4.0   ESTIMATION AND MEASUREMENT

Skill 4.1   Understand and use standard units of length, temperature, weight, and capacity in the U.S. measurement system

Measurements of length (English system)

12 inches (in)	=	1 foot (ft)
3 feet (ft)	=	1 yard (yd)
1760 yards (yd)	=	1 mile (mi)

Measurements of length (Metric system)

1 kilometer (km)	=	1000 meters (m)
1 hectometer (hm)	=	100 meters (m)
1 decameter (dam)	=	10 meters (m)
1 meter (m)	=	1 meter (m)
1 decimeter (dm)	=	1/10 meter (m)
1 centimeter (cm)	=	1/100 meter (m)
1 millimeter (mm)	=	1/1000 meter (m)

Conversion of length from English to Metric

1 inch	=	2.54 centimeters
1 foot	≈	30 centimeters
1 yard	≈	0.9 meters
1 mile	≈	1.6 kilometers

Measurements of weight (English system)

28 grams (g)	=	1 ounce (oz)
16 ounces (oz)	=	1 pound (lb)
2000 pounds (lb)	=	1 ton (t)

Measurements of weight (Metric system)

1 kilogram (kg)	=	1000 grams (g)
1 gram (g)	=	1 gram (g)
1 milligram (mg)	=	1/1000 gram (g)

Conversion of weight from English to Metric

1 ounce	≈	28 grams
1 pound	≈	0.45 kilograms
	≈	454 grams

Measurement of volume (English system)

8 fluid ounces (oz)	=	1 cup (c)
2 cups (c)	=	1 pint (pt)
2 pints (pt)	=	1 quart (qt)
4 quarts (qt)	=	1 gallon (gal)

Measurement of volume (Metric system)

1 kiloliter (kl)	=	1000 liters (l)
1 liter (l)	=	1 liter (l)
1 milliliter (ml)	=	1/1000 liters (ml)

Conversion of volume from English to Metric

1 teaspoon (tsp)	≈	5 milliliters
1 fluid ounce	≈	15 milliliters
1 cup	≈	0.24 liters
1 pint	≈	0.47 liters
1 quart	≈	0.95 liters
1 gallon	≈	3.8 liters

Measurement of time

1 minute	=	60 seconds
1 hour	=	60 minutes
1 day	=	24 hours
1 week	=	7 days
1 year	=	365 days
1 century	=	100 years

Note: (') represents feet and (") represents inches.

Skill 4.2   Measure length, perimeter, area, and volume

The **perimeter** of any polygon is the sum of the lengths of the sides.

The **area** of a polygon is the number of square units covered by the figure.

FIGURE	AREA FORMULA	PERIMETER FORMULA
Square	Side x Side	4(side)
Rectangle	Length x Width	2(Length + Width)
Triangle	$\frac{1}{2}bh$ (b = base, h = height)	$a + b + c$ (where a, b, and c are legs of the triangle)
Parallelogram	bh	sum of the lengths of the sides
Trapezoid	$\frac{1}{2}h(a + b)$ (where a and b are the bases)	sum of the lengths of the sides

Perimeter of a Polygon

Example: A farmer has a piece of land shaped as shown below. He wishes to fence this land. The estimated cost is $25 per linear foot. What is the total cost of fencing this property to the nearest foot?

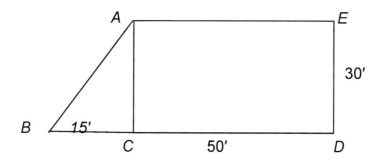

From the right triangle ABC, AC = 30 and BC = 15.

Since $(AB)^2 = (AC)^2 + (BC)^2$
$(AB)^2 = (30)^2 + (15)^2$

So, $\sqrt{(AB)^2} = AB = \sqrt{30^2 + 15^2} = \sqrt{1125} = 33.5410$ feet

To the nearest foot, AB = 34 feet.

Perimeter of the piece of land = $AB + BC + CD + DE + EA$

= 34 + 15 + 50 + 30 + 50 = 179 feet

Cost of fencing = $25 x 179 = $4, 475

Area of a Polygon

Example: What is the cost of carpeting a rectangular office that measures 12 feet by 15 feet if the carpet costs $12.50 per square yard?

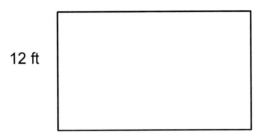

12 ft

15 ft

This is a basic area problem. To solve this problem you must first determine the area of the office. The area of a rectangle is the *length* times the *width*.

Substitute the given values in the equation $A = lw$

$$A = (12 \text{ ft})(15 \text{ ft})$$

$$A = 180 \text{ ft}^2$$

The problem asked you to determine the cost of carpet at $12.50 per square yard.

First, you need to convert 180 ft.^{2} into yards^2.

1 yd. = 3 ft.

(1 yard)(1 yard) = (3 feet)(3 feet)

$1 \text{ yd}^2 = 9 \text{ ft}^2$

Hence, $180 \text{ ft}^2 = 20 \text{ yd}^2$ $(180 \div 9)$

The carpet costs $12.50 per square yard; thus, the cost of carpeting the office is $12.50 x 20 yd^2 = $250.

Example: Find the area of a parallelogram with bases 6.5 cm long and altitude 3.7 cm long. (note: the altitude is the line perpendicular to the bases)

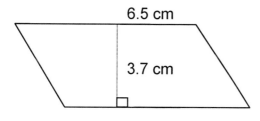

6.5 cm

3.7 cm

$$A_{parallelogram} = bh$$
$$= (3.7)(6.5)$$
$$= 24.05 \text{ cm}^2$$

Example: Find the area of this triangle.

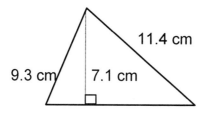

11.4 cm

9.3 cm   7.1 cm

16.8 cm

$$A_{triangle} = \tfrac{1}{2}bh$$
$$= 0.5\,(16.8)\,(7.1)$$
$$= 59.64 \text{ cm}^2$$

Example: Find the area of this trapezoid.

17.5 cm

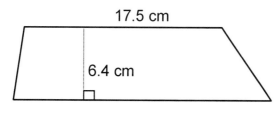

6.4 cm

23.7 cm

The area of a trapezoid equals one-half the sum of the bases times the altitude.

$$A_{trapezoid} = \tfrac{1}{2}h(b_1 + b_2)$$
$$= 0.5\,(6.4)\,(17.5 + 23.7)$$
$$= 131.84 \text{ cm}^2$$

Circles

The distance around a circle is the **circumference**. The ratio of the circumference to the diameter is represented by the Greek letter pi (π).

$$\pi \approx 3.14 \approx \frac{22}{7}$$

The formula used to find the circumference of a circle is $C = 2\pi r$ or $C = \pi d$ where r is the radius of the circle and d is the diameter.

The formula used to find the **area** of a circle is $A = \pi r^2$.

Example: Find the circumference and area of a circle whose radius is 7 meters.

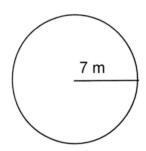

C = $2\pi r$
= 2(3.14)(7)
= 43.96 m

A = πr^2
= 3.14(7)(7)
= 153.86 m^2

The following are formulas used to compute **Volume** and **Surface area**:

FIGURE	VOLUME	TOTAL SURFACE AREA
Right Cylinder	$\pi r^2 h$	$2\pi rh + 2\pi r^2$
Right Cone	$\dfrac{\pi r^2 h}{3}$	$\pi r\sqrt{r^2 + h^2} + \pi r^2$
Sphere	$\dfrac{4}{3}\pi r^3$	$4\pi r^2$
Rectangular Solid	LWH	$2LW + 2WH + 2LH$

FIGURE	LATERAL AREA	TOTAL AREA	VOLUME
Regular Pyramid	1/2Pl	1/2Pl+B	1/3Bh

P = Perimeter
h = height
B = Area of Base
l = slant height

Example: What is the volume of a shoe box with a length of 35 cm, a width of 20 cm, and a height of 15 cm?

Volume of a rectangular solid
= Length x Width x Height
= 35 x 20 x 15
= 10500 cm^3

Example: A water company is trying to decide whether to use traditional cylindrical paper cups or to offer conical paper cups since both cost the same amount. The traditional cups are 8 cm wide and 14 cm high. The conical cups are 12 cm wide and 19 cm high. The company will use the cup that holds the most water.

Draw and label a sketch of each.

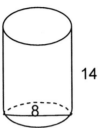 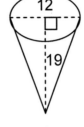

$V = \pi r^2 h$ $\qquad$ $V = \dfrac{\pi r^2 h}{3}$ $\qquad$ 1. write formula

$V = \pi (4)^2 (14)$ $\qquad$ $V = \dfrac{1}{3} \pi (6)^2 (19)$ $\qquad$ 2. substitute

$V = 703.717 \text{ cm}^3$ $\qquad$ $V = 716.283 \text{ cm}^3$ $\qquad$ 3. solve

The choice should be the conical cup, because it has a greater volume and can hold more water.

Example: How much material is needed to make a basketball that has a diameter of 15 inches? How much air is needed to fill the basketball?

Draw and label a sketch.

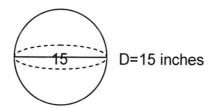 D=15 inches

The amount of material needed is equal to the surface area and the amount of air needed is equal to the volume.

Total surface area   Volume

$\text{TSA} = 4\pi r^2$ $V = \dfrac{4}{3}\pi r^3$ 1. write formula

$\qquad = 4\pi(7.5)^2$ $= \dfrac{4}{3}\pi(7.5)^3$ 2. substitute

$\qquad = 706.858 \text{ in}^2$ $= 1767.1459 \text{ in}^3$ 3. solve

Skill 4.3   Understand and use estimates of time to plan and achieve work-related objectives

Since you cannot accurately predict what will happen in the future, you can only estimate how much of your time will be available for any given activity or task. Estimating time and planning for work-related objectives involves estimating both the time the objective will take and the time you will have available to complete the objective.

Example: Your boss has asked you to prepare a report on current research on reading interventions. She wants to know when you think you can have this report to her.

Solution: You first estimate how long you think it will take to create the report:

Research:	5 hours
Outline:	1 hour
Draft:	3 hours
Written report:	1 hour
Review and corrections:	<u>1 hour</u>
Total	11 hours

Then, you need to figure how this time requirement fits into your current schedule. You work 8 hours per day. Of this, you estimate that 20% of your time is taken up with administrative tasks. You allow 10% for interruptions (e.g., phone calls and visitors). You also have another project, which requires at least 40% of your time. Thus, you can represent your available time as follows.

$$8 - (.2)(8) - (.1)(8) - (.4)(8) =$$
$$8 - 1.6 - 0.8 - 3.2 = 2.4$$

Therefore, you are left with 2.4 hours each day to work on the report. Since you estimate that the report will need 11 hours you estimate that you will need 5 days to complete the report and turn it in to your boss.

11 hours ÷ 2.4 hours/day = 4.6 days

Skill 4.4   Estimate the results of problems involving addition, subtraction, multiplication, and division prior to computation

Regrouping to Estimate Differences

We can estimate the difference of two numbers by first rounding the numbers and then subtracting the rounded numbers. When subtracting two rounded numbers, one rounded up and the other rounded down, we can improve our estimate by regrouping. For example, when estimating the difference of 540 and 355, we round 540 down to 500 and 355 up to 400. Thus, our estimated difference is 500 minus 400, or 100. Note that we rounded 540 down by 40 and 355 up by 45. Thus, the total amount of rounding is 85. Rounding 85 up to 100 and adding this rounded sum to 100 (our original estimate) gives us a final estimated difference of 200. This is closer to the actual difference of 185 (540 – 355). The regrouping method of estimation only works when we round the two numbers in opposite directions.

Front End Estimation

While we can add or subtract rounded numbers to estimate sums and differences, another method, front-end estimation, is simpler and usually delivers results that are just as accurate. Front-end estimation is an elementary form of estimation of sums and differences. To estimate a sum or difference by front-end estimation, we add or subtract only the two highest place values and filling the remaining place values with zeroes.

Example: Estimate 4987 + 3512 by front-end estimation.

The estimated sum is 8400 (4900 + 3500).

Note that we do not round the numbers, but merely drop the digits after the two highest place values. In other words, we convert 4987 to 4900, not 5000.

Example: Estimate 3894 – 617 by front-end estimation.

The estimated difference is 3200 (3800 – 600).

Note that because 617 does not have a digit in the thousands place and 3894 does, we convert 617 to 600, not 610.

Applied Estimation Example

Janet goes into a store to purchase a CD on sale for $13.95. While shopping, she sees two pairs of shoes, priced $19.95 and $14.50. She only has $50. Can she purchase everything?

Solve by rounding:

$19.95→$20.00
$14.50→$15.00
$13.95→$14.00
        $49.00   Yes, she can purchase the CD and the shoes.

COMPETENCY 5.0   STATISTICAL PRINCIPLES

Skill 5.1   Perform arithmetic operations with basic statistical data related to test scores (e.g., averages, ratios, proportions, and percentile scores)

The arithmetic **mean** (or average) of a set of numbers is the *sum* of the numbers given, *divided* by the number of items in the set.

Example: Find the mean of the following numbers. Round to the nearest tenth.

24.6, 57.3, 44.1, 39.8, 64.5

The sum is 230.3

The mean is 230.3/5

= 46.06, rounded to 46.1 (nearest tenth)

The **median** of a set is the middle number. To calculate the median, we must arrange the terms in order. If there is an even number of terms, the median is the mean of the two middle terms.

Example: Find the median.

12. 14. 27. 3. 13. 7. 17.   12. 22. 6.   16

Rearrange the terms.
3, 6, 7, 12, 12, 13, 14,   16, 17, 22, 27
Since there are 11 numbers, the middle would be the sixth number or 13.

The **mode** of a set of numbers is the number that occurs with the greatest frequency. A set can have no mode if each term appears exactly one time. Similarly, there can also be more than one mode.

Example: Find the mode.

26, 15, 37, **26,** 35, **26,** 15

15 appears twice, but 26 appears 3 times; therefore the mode is 26.

The **range** is the difference between the highest and lowest values in the data set.

Example: Given the ungrouped data below, calculate the mean and range.

15	22	28	25	34	38
18	25	30	33	19	23

Mean ($\overline{X}$) = 25.8333333
Range: $38 - 15 = 23$

A **ratio** is a comparison of 2 numbers. If a class had 11 boys and 14 girls, we can write the ratio of boys to girls in 3 ways:

$$11:14 \quad \text{or} \quad 11 \text{ to } 14 \quad \text{or} \quad \frac{11}{14}$$

The ratio of girls to boys is:

$$14:11, \ 14 \text{ to } 11 \text{ or } \frac{14}{11}$$

We should reduce ratios when possible. A ratio of 12 cats to 18 dogs reduces to 2:3, 2 to 3, or $2/3$.

Note: Read ratio questions carefully. Given a group of 6 adults and 5 children, the ratio of children to the *entire group* would be 5:11.

A **proportion** is an equation in which one fraction is set equal to another. To solve the proportion, multiply each numerator by the other fraction's denominator. Set these two products equal to each other and solve the resulting equation. This is called **cross-multiplying** the proportion.

Example: $\dfrac{4}{15} = \dfrac{x}{60}$ is a proportion.

To solve, cross multiply.

$(4)(60) = (15)(x)$

$240 = 15x$

$16 = x$

Example: $\dfrac{x+3}{3x+4} = \dfrac{2}{5}$ is a proportion.

To solve, cross multiply.

$5(x+3) = 2(3x+4)$

$5x + 15 = 6x + 8$

$7 = x$

Example: $\dfrac{x+2}{8} = \dfrac{2}{x-4}$ is another proportion.

To solve, cross multiply.

$(x+2)(x-4) = 8(2)$

$x^2 - 2x - 8 = 16$

$x^2 - 2x - 24 = 0$

$(x-6)(x+4) = 0$

$x = 6$ or $x = {}^{-}4$

We can use **proportions** to solve word problems that involve comparisons of relationships. Some situations include scale drawings and maps, similar polygons, speed, time and distance, cost, and comparison shopping.

Example 1:   Which is the better buy, 6 items for $1.29 or 8 of the same items for $1.69?

Find the unit price.

$\dfrac{6}{1.29} = \dfrac{1}{x}$ $\dfrac{8}{1.69} = \dfrac{1}{x}$

$6x = 1.29$ $8x = 1.69$

$x = 0.215$ $x = 0.21125$

Thus, 8 items for $1.69 is the better buy (lower unit price).

Example: A car travels 125 miles in 2.5 hours. How far will it go in 6 hours?

Write a proportion comparing the distance and time.

$$\frac{miles}{hours} \qquad \frac{125}{2.5} = \frac{x}{6}$$

$2.5x = 750$
$x = 300$

Thus, the car can travel 300 miles in 6 hours.

Example: The scale on a map is $\frac{3}{4}$ inch = 6 miles. What is the actual distance between two cities if they are $1\frac{1}{2}$ inches apart on the map?

Write a proportion comparing the scale to the actual distance.

$$\text{scale} \qquad \text{actual}$$
$$\frac{\frac{3}{4}}{1\frac{1}{2}} = \frac{6}{x}$$
$$\frac{3}{4}x = 1\frac{1}{2} \times 6$$
$$\frac{3}{4}x = 9$$
$$x = 12$$

Thus, the actual distance between the cities is 12 miles.

Skill 5.2 **Understand basic principles of probability and predict likely outcomes based on data provided (e.g., estimate the likelihood that an event will occur)**

In probability, the **sample space** is a list of all possible outcomes of an experiment. For example, the sample space of tossing two coins is the set {HH, HT, TT, TH}, the sample space of rolling a six-sided die is the set {1, 2, 3, 4, 5, 6}, and the sample space of measuring the height of students in a class is the set of all real numbers {R}. **Probability** measures the chances of an event occurring. The probability of an event that *must* occur, a certain event, is **one**. When no outcome is favorable, the probability of an impossible event is **zero**.

$$P(event) = \frac{number\ of\ favorable\ outcomes}{number\ of\ possible\ outcomes}$$

Example: Given one die with faces numbered 1 - 6, the probability of tossing an even number on one throw of the die is 3/6 or ½, since there are 3 favorable outcomes (even-numbered faces) and a total of 6 possible outcomes (faces).

Example: We roll a fair die...

a) Find the probability of rolling an even number
b) Find the probability of rolling a number less than three

a) The sample space is S = {1, 2, 3, 4, 5, 6} and the event is the possible even numbers E = {2, 4, 6}.

Hence, the probability of rolling an even number is

$$p(E) = \frac{n(E)}{n(S)} = \frac{3}{6} = \frac{1}{2} \text{ or } 0.5$$

b) A = {1, 2} represents the event of rolling a number less than three.

Hence, the probability of rolling a number less than three is

$$p(A) = \frac{n(A)}{n(S)} = \frac{2}{6} = \frac{1}{3} \text{ or } 0.33$$

Example: A class has thirty students. Of the thirty students, twenty-four are males. Assuming all the students have the same chance of selection, find the probability of selecting a female. (We only select one person.)

The number of females in the class is

$$30 - 24 = 6$$

Hence, the probability of selecting a female is

$$p(female) = \frac{6}{30} = \frac{1}{5} \text{ or } 0.2$$

If A and B are **independent** events then the outcome of event A does not affect the outcome of event B or vice versa. We use the multiplication to find joint probability.

$$P(A \text{ and } B) = P(A) \times P(B)$$

Example: The probability that a patient is allergic to aspirin is 0.30. If the probability of a patient having a window in his/her room is 0.40, find the probability that the patient is allergic to aspirin and has a window in his/her room.

Defining the events: A = The patient is allergic to aspirin.
B = The patient has a window in his/her room.

Events A and B are independent, hence
p(A and B) = p(A) · p(B)
= (0.30) (0.40)
= 0.12 or 12%

Example: Given a jar containing 10 marbles, 3 red, 5 black, and 2 white. What is the probability of drawing a red marble and then a white marble if we return the marble to the jar after choosing?

3/10 X 2/10 = 6/100 = 3/50 or 0.06 or 6%

When the outcome of the first event affects the outcome of the second event, the events are **dependent.** Any two events that are not independent are dependent. This is also known as conditional probability.

Probability of (A and B) = P(A) × P(B, given A)

Example: We draw two cards from a deck of 52 cards, without replacement. In other words, we do not return the first card we select to the deck before drawing the second card. What is the probability of drawing two diamonds?

A = drawing a diamond first
B = drawing a diamond second

P(A) = drawing a diamond first
P(B) = drawing a diamond second

P(A) = 13/52 = 1/4   P(B) = 12/52 = 4/17

(PA+B) = 1/4 X 14/17 = 7/34

Example: A class of ten students has six males and four females. If we select two students to represent the class, find the probability that

a) the first is a male and the second is a female.
b) the first is a female and the second is a male.
c) both are females.
d) both are males.

Define the events:

F = a female is selected to represent the class
M = a male is selected to represent the class

F/M = a female is selected after a male has been selected

M/F = a male is selected after a female has been selected

a)   Since F and M are dependent events, it follows that
P(M and F) = P(M) · P(F/M)
$$= \frac{6}{10} \times \frac{4}{9} = \frac{3}{5} \times \frac{4}{9} = \frac{12}{45}$$

$P(F/M) = \dfrac{4}{9}$ instead of , $\dfrac{4}{10}$ since the selection of a male first changed the sample space from ten to nine students.

b)   P(F and M) = P(F) · P(M/F)
$$= \frac{4}{10} \times \frac{6}{9} = \frac{2}{5} \times \frac{2}{3} = \frac{4}{15}$$

c) $P(F \text{ and } F) = p(F) \cdot p(F/F)$

$$= \frac{4}{10} \times \frac{3}{9} = \frac{2}{5} \times \frac{1}{3} = \frac{2}{15}$$

d) $P(\text{both are males}) = p(M \text{ and } M)$

$$= \frac{6}{10} \times \frac{5}{9} = \frac{30}{90} = \frac{1}{3}$$

Odds are the ratio of the number of favorable outcomes to the number of unfavorable outcomes. The sum of the favorable outcomes and the unfavorable outcomes will always equal the total possible outcomes. For example, given a bag of 12 red and 7 green marbles compute the odds of randomly selecting a red marble.

$$\text{Odds of red} = \frac{12}{19} : \frac{7}{19} \text{ or } 12{:}7.$$

$$\text{Odds of not getting red} = \frac{7}{19} : \frac{12}{19} \text{ or } 7{:}12.$$

In the case of flipping a coin, it is equally likely that the coin will land on heads or tails. Thus, the odds of tossing a head are 1:1. These are even odds.

Skill 5.3   **Interpret the meaning of stanine scores and percentiles (e.g., determine how individuals performed relative to other students)**

Percentiles divide data into 100 equal parts. A person whose score falls in the 65th percentile has outperformed 65 percent of all test takers. This does not mean that the person scored 65 percent out of 100 nor does it mean that he or she answered 65 percent of the questions correctly.

Stanine, or "standard nine," scores combine the understandability of percentages with the properties of the normal curve of probability. Stanines divide the bell curve into nine sections, the largest of which, the "fifth stanine," stretches from the 40th to the 60th percentile.

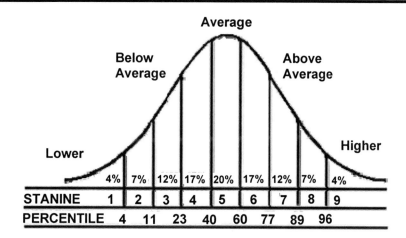

Quartiles divide the data into 4 parts. First find the median of the data set (Q2), then find the median of the upper (Q3) and lower (Q1) halves of the data set. If there are an odd number of values in the data set, include the median value in both halves when finding quartile values. For example, given the data set {1, 4, 9, 16, 25, 36, 49, 64, 81} first find the median value, which is 25. This is the second quartile. Since there are an odd number of values in the data set (9), we include the median in both halves.

To find the quartile values, we must find the medians of {1, 4, 9, 16, 25} and {25, 36, 49, 64, 81}. Since each of these subsets had an odd number of elements (5), we use the middle value. Thus the first quartile value is 9 and the third quartile value is 49. If the data set had an even number of elements, average the middle two values. The quartile values are always either one data point or exactly half way between two data points.

Example: Given the following set of data, find the percentile of the score 104.
70, 72, 82, 83, 84, 87, 100, 104, 108, 109, 110, 115

Find the percentage of scores below 104.

7/12 of the scores are less than 104. This is 58.333%; therefore, the score of 104 is in the 58th percentile.

Example: Find the first, second, and third quartile of the following data set.
6, 7, 8, 9, 10, 12, 13, 14, 15, 16, 18, 23, 24, 25, 27, 29, 30, 33, 34, 37

Quartile 1: The 1st Quartile is the median of the lower half of the data set, which is 11.

Quartile 2: The median of the data set is the 2nd Quartile, which is 17.

Quartile 3: The 3rd Quartile is the median of the upper half of the data set, which is 28.

COMPETENCY 6.0   COMPUTATION & PROBLEM SOLVING

Skill 6.1   Add, subtract, multiply, and divide with whole numbers

Properties are rules that apply for addition, subtraction, multiplication, or division of real numbers. These properties are:

Commutative: You can change the order of the terms or factors as follows.

For addition: $a + b = b + a$
For multiplication: $ab = ba$

Associative: You can regroup the terms as you like.

For addition: $a + (b + c) = (a + b) + c$
For multiplication: $a(bc) = (ab)c$

This rule does not apply for division and subtraction.

Example: $(^-2 + 7) + 5 = ^-2 + (7 + 5)$
$5 + 5 = ^-2 + 12 = 10$

Example: $(3 \times ^-7) \times 5 = 3 \times (^-7 \times 5)$
$^-21 \times 5 = 3 \times ^-35 = ^-105$

Identity: A number that when added to a term results in that same number (additive identity); a number that when multiplied by a term results in that same number (multiplicative identity).

For addition: $a + 0 = a$ (zero is additive identity)
For multiplication: $a \times 1 = a$ (one is multiplicative)

Example: $17 + 0 = 17$

Example: $^-34 \times 1 = ^-34$

The product of any number and one is that number.

Distributive: This technique allows us to operate on terms within parentheses without first performing operations within the parentheses. This is especially helpful when we cannot combine terms within the parentheses.

$a (b + c) = ab + ac$

Example: $6 \times (\bar{}4 + 9) = (6 \times \bar{}4) + (6 \times 9)$
$6 \times 5 = \bar{}24 + 54 = 30$

To multiply a sum by a number, multiply each addend by the number, then add the products.

Addition of whole numbers

Example: At the end of a day of shopping, a shopper had $24 remaining in his wallet. He spent $45 on various goods. How much money did the shopper have at the beginning of the day?

The total amount of money the shopper started with is the sum of the amount spent and the amount remaining at the end of the day.

$$\begin{array}{r} 24 \\ + \ 45 \\ \hline 69 \end{array}$$ The original total was $69.

Example: The winner of a race took 1 hr. 58 min. 12 sec. on the first half of the race and 2 hr. 9 min. 57 sec. on the second half of the race. What was the winner's total time?

1 hr. 58 min. 12 sec.
+ 2 hr. 9 min. 57 sec.   Add these numbers
3 hr. 67 min. 69 sec.
+   1 min - 60 sec.   Change 60 seconds to 1min.
3 hr. 68 min. 9 sec.
+ 1 hr.-60 min.   .   Change 60 minutes to 1 hr.
4 hr. 8 min. 9 sec. ← Final answer

Subtraction of Whole Numbers

Example: At the end of his shift, a cashier has $96 in the cash register. At the beginning of his shift, he had $15. How much money did the cashier collect during his shift?

The total collected is the difference of the ending amount and the starting amount.

$$\begin{array}{r} 96 \\ - \ 15 \\ \hline 81 \end{array}$$ The total collected was $81.

Multiplication of whole numbers

Multiplication is one of the four basic number operations. In simple terms, multiplication is the addition of a number to itself a certain number of times. For example, 4 multiplied by 3 is the equal to 4 + 4 + 4 or 3 + 3 + 3 +3. Another way of conceptualizing multiplication is to think in terms of groups. For example, if we have 4 groups of 3 students, the total number of students is 4 multiplied by 3. We call the solution to a multiplication problem the product.

The basic algorithm for whole number multiplication begins with aligning the numbers by place value with the number containing more places on top.

$$\begin{array}{r} 172 \\ \times\ \ 43 \end{array} \longrightarrow$$ Note that we placed 122 on top because it has more places than 43 has.

Next, we multiply the ones place of the second number by each place value of the top number sequentially.

$$\begin{array}{r} (2) \\ 172 \\ \times\ \ 43 \\ \hline 516 \end{array} \longrightarrow$$ {3 x 2 = 6, 3 x 7 = 21, 3 x 1 = 3}
Note that we had to carry a 2 to the hundreds column because 3 x 7 = 21. Note also that we add, not multiply, carried numbers to the product.

Next, we multiply the number in the tens place of the second number by each place value of the top number sequentially. Because we are multiplying by a number in the tens place, we place a zero at the end of this product.

$$\begin{array}{r} (2) \\ 172 \\ \times\ \ 43 \\ \hline 516 \\ 6880 \end{array} \longrightarrow$$ {4 x 2 = 8, 4 x 7 = 28, 4 x 1 = 4}

Finally, to determine the final product we add the two partial products.

$$\begin{array}{r} 172 \\ \times\ \ 43 \\ \hline 516 \\ +\ 6880 \\ \hline 7396 \end{array} \longrightarrow$$ The product of 172 and 43 is 7396.

Example: A student buys 4 boxes of crayons. Each box contains 16 crayons. How many total crayons does the student have?

The total number of crayons is 16 x 4.

$$
\begin{array}{r}
16 \\
\times\ 4 \\
\hline
64
\end{array}
$$
→ Total number of crayons equals 64.

Division of whole numbers

Division, the inverse of multiplication, is another of the four basic number operations. When we divide one number by another, we determine how many times we can multiply the divisor (number divided by) before we exceed the number we are dividing (dividend). For example, 8 divided by 2 equals 4 because we can multiply 2 four times to reach 8 (2 x 4 = 8 or 2 + 2 + 2 + 2 = 8). Using the grouping conceptualization we used with multiplication, we can divide 8 into 4 groups of 2 or 2 groups of 4. We call the answer to a division problem the quotient.

If the divisor does not divide evenly into the dividend, we express the leftover amount either as a remainder or as a fraction with the divisor as the denominator. For example, 9 divided by 2 equals 4 with a remainder of 1 or 4 ½.

The basic algorithm for division is long division. We start by representing the quotient as follows.

$14\overline{)293}$ → 14 is the divisor and 293 is the dividend.

This represents 293 ÷ 14.

Next, we divide the divisor into the dividend starting from the left.

$14\overline{)293}^{\,2}$ → 14 divides into 29 two times with a remainder.

Next, we multiply the partial quotient by the divisor, subtract this value from the first digits of the dividend, and bring down the remaining dividend digits to complete the number.

$$
\begin{array}{r}
2\ \ \ \\
14\overline{)293} \\
-28\ \ \\
\hline
13\ \
\end{array}
$$
→ 2 x 14 = 28, 29 – 28 = 1, and bringing down the 3 yields 13.

Finally, we divide again (the divisor into the remaining value) and repeat the preceding process. The number left after the subtraction represents the remainder.

$$14\overline{)293}$$

```
        20
  14)293
   - 28
      13
    -  0
      13  ──────▶
```

The final quotient is 20 with a remainder of 13. We can also represent this quotient as 20 13/14.

Example: Each box of apples contains 24 apples. How many boxes must a grocer purchase to supply a group of 252 people with one apple each?

The grocer needs 252 apples. Because he must buy apples in groups of 24, we divide 252 by 24 to determine how many boxes he needs to buy.

```
         10
   24)252
      -24
        12 ──────▶  The quotient is 10 with a remainder of 12.
       - 0
        12
```

Thus, the grocer needs 10 boxes plus 12 more apples. Therefore, the minimum number of boxes the grocer can purchase is 11.

Example: At his job, John gets paid $20 for every hour he works. If John made $940 in a week, how many hours did he work?

This is a division problem. To determine the number of hours John worked, we divide the total amount made ($940) by the hourly rate of pay ($20). Thus, the number of hours worked equals 940 divided by 20.

```
          47
   20)940
      -80
      140
     -140
        0  ──────▶
```

20 divides into 940, 47 times with no remainder.

John worked 47 hours.

Skill 6.2   Add and subtract with positive and negative numbers

Addition

If a and b are positive, they are added as whole numbers.

Example: $32 + 45 = 77$

If a and b are negative, then $(-a) + (-b) = -(a + b)$.

Example: $(-104) + (-22) = -(104 + 22) = -126$

If a is positive and b is negative and $|a| < |b|$, then $a + (-b) = a - b$.

Example: $45 + (-30) = 45 - 30 = 15$

If a is positive and b is negative and $|a| < |b|$, then $a + (-b) = -(b - a)$.

Example: $15 + (-26) = -(26 - 15) = -9$

Subtraction

For any integers a and b, $a - b = a + (-b)$; i.e. add the opposite.

Examples:
$$22 - 70 = 22 + (-70) = -48$$
$$18 - (-10) = 18 + (10) = 28$$
$$-33 - (-9) = -33 + (9) = -24$$

Skill 6.3   Add, subtract, multiply, and divide with fractions, decimals, and percentages

Addition and Subtraction of Decimals

When adding and subtracting decimals, we align the numbers by place value as we do with whole numbers. After adding or subtracting each column, we bring the decimal down, placing it in the same location as in the numbers added or subtracted.

Example: Find the sum of 152.3 and 36.342.

$$
\begin{array}{r}
152.300 \\
+\ \ 36.342 \\
\hline
188.642
\end{array}
$$

Note that we placed two zeroes after the final place value in 152.3 to clarify the column addition.

Example: Find the difference of 152.3 and 36.342.

$$
\begin{array}{r}
2\ 9\ 10 \\
152.\cancel{300} \\
-\ \ 36.342 \\
\hline
58
\end{array}
\qquad\longrightarrow\qquad
\begin{array}{r}
(4)11(12) \\
1\cancel{52.300} \\
-\ \ 36.342 \\
\hline
115.958
\end{array}
$$

Note how we borrowed to subtract from the zeroes in the hundredths and thousandths place of 152.300.

Multiplication of Decimals

When multiplying decimal numbers, we multiply exactly as with whole numbers and place the decimal moving in from the left the total number of decimal places contained in the two numbers multiplied. For example, when multiplying 1.5 and 2.35, we place the decimal in the product 3 places in from the left (3.525).

Example: Find the product of 3.52 and 4.1.

$$
\begin{array}{r}
3.52 \\
\times\ \ 4.1 \\
\hline
352 \\
+\ \ 14080 \\
\hline
14432
\end{array}
$$

Note that there are 3 total decimal places in the two numbers.

We place the decimal 3 places in from the left.

Thus, the final product is 14.432.

Example: A shopper has 5 one-dollar bills, 6 quarters, 3 nickels, and 4 pennies in his pocket. How much money does he have?

$$
\begin{array}{cccc}
& 3 & & \\
5 \times \$1.00 = \$5.00 & \$0.25 & \$0.05 & \$0.01 \\
& \times\ \ 6 & \times\ \ 3 & \times\ \ 4 \\
\hline
& \$1.50 & \$0.15 & \$0.04
\end{array}
$$

Note the placement of the decimals in the multiplication products. Thus, the total amount of money in the shopper's pocket is:

$$
\begin{array}{r}
\$5.00 \\
1.50 \\
0.15 \\
+\ 0.04 \\
\hline
\$6.69
\end{array}
$$

Division of Decimals

When dividing decimal numbers, we first remove the decimal in the divisor by moving the decimal in the dividend the same number of spaces to the right. For example, when dividing 1.45 into 5.3 we convert the numbers to 145 and 530 and perform normal whole number division.

Example: Find the quotient of 5.3 divided by 1.45.
Convert to 145 and 530.

Divide.

$$
\begin{array}{r}
3 \\
145\overline{)530} \\
-\ 435 \\
\hline
95
\end{array}
\qquad\longrightarrow\qquad
\begin{array}{r}
3.65 \\
145\overline{)530.00} \\
-\ 435 \\
\hline
950 \\
-\ 870 \\
\hline
800
\end{array}
\qquad\longrightarrow
$$

Note that we insert the decimal to continue division.

Because one of the numbers divided contained one decimal place, we round the quotient to one decimal place. Thus, the final quotient is 3.7.

Operating with Percents

Example: 5 is what percent of 20?

This is the same as converting $\dfrac{5}{20}$ to % form.

$$\frac{5}{20} \times \frac{100}{1} = \frac{5}{1} \times \frac{5}{1} = 25\%$$

Example: There are 64 dogs in the kennel. 48 are collies. What percentage of the dogs are collies?

Restate the problem.   48 is what percent of 64?
Write an equation. $48 = n \times 64$
Solve. $\frac{48}{64} = n$

$n = \frac{3}{4} = 75\%$

75% of the dogs are collies.

Example: The auditorium was filled to 90% capacity. There were 558 seats occupied. What is the capacity of the auditorium?

Restate the problem.   90% of what number is 558?
Write an equation. $0.9n = 558$
Solve. $n = \frac{558}{.9}$

$n = 620$

The capacity of the auditorium is 620 people.

Example: A pair of shoes costs $42. Sales tax is 6%. What is the total cost of the shoes?

Restate the problem.   What is 6% of 42?
Write an equation. $n = 0.06 \times 42$
Solve. $n = 2.52$

Add the sales tax to the cost. $42.00 + $2.52 = $44.52

The total cost of the shoes, including sales tax, is $44.52.

Addition and subtraction of fractions

<u>Key Points</u>

1. You need a common denominator in order to add and subtract reduced and improper fractions.

    Example: $\dfrac{1}{3} + \dfrac{7}{3} = \dfrac{1+7}{3} = \dfrac{8}{3} = 2\dfrac{2}{3}$

    Example: $\dfrac{4}{12} + \dfrac{6}{12} - \dfrac{3}{12} = \dfrac{4+6-3}{12} = \dfrac{7}{12}$

2. Adding an integer and a fraction of the <u>same</u> sign results directly in a mixed fraction.

    Example: $2 + \dfrac{2}{3} = 2\dfrac{2}{3}$

    Example: $^-2 - \dfrac{3}{4} = {}^- 2\dfrac{3}{4}$

3. Adding an integer and a fraction with different signs involves the following steps.

    - find a common denominator
    - add or subtract as needed
    - change to a mixed fraction if possible

    Example: $2 - \dfrac{1}{3} = \dfrac{2 \times 3 - 1}{3} = \dfrac{6-1}{3} = \dfrac{5}{3} = 1\dfrac{2}{3}$

Example: Add $7\dfrac{3}{8} + 5\dfrac{2}{7}$

Add the whole numbers; add the fractions and combine the two results:

$$7\dfrac{3}{8} + 5\dfrac{2}{7} = (7+5) + (\dfrac{3}{8} + \dfrac{2}{7})$$

$$= 12 + \dfrac{(7 \times 3) + (8 \times 2)}{56} \quad \text{(LCM of 8 and 7)}$$

$$= 12 + \dfrac{21+16}{56} = 12 + \dfrac{37}{56} = 12\dfrac{37}{56}$$

Example: Perform the operation.

$$\frac{2}{3} - \frac{5}{6}$$

We first find the LCM of 3 and 6 which is 6.

$$\frac{2 \times 2}{3 \times 2} - \frac{5}{6} \rightarrow \frac{4-5}{6} = \frac{^-1}{6}$$

Example: $^-7\dfrac{1}{4} + 2\dfrac{7}{8}$

$$^-7\frac{1}{4} + 2\frac{7}{8} = (^-7 + 2) + (\frac{^-1}{4} + \frac{7}{8})$$

$$= (^-5) + \frac{(^-2+7)}{8} \quad = (^-5) + (\frac{5}{8})$$

$$= (^-5) + \frac{5}{8} = \frac{^-5 \times 8}{1 \times 8} + \frac{5}{8} = \frac{^-40 + 5}{8}$$

$$= \frac{^-35}{8} = {}^-4\frac{3}{8}$$

Divide 35 by 8 to get 4, remainder 3.

Caution: A common error is...

$$^-7\frac{1}{4} + 2\frac{7}{8} = {}^-7\frac{2}{8} + 2\frac{7}{8} = {}^-5\frac{9}{8} \qquad \text{Wrong.}$$

It is correct to add -7 and 2 to get -5, but adding $\dfrac{2}{8} + \dfrac{7}{8} = \dfrac{9}{8}$

is wrong. It should have been $\dfrac{^-2}{8} + \dfrac{7}{8} = \dfrac{5}{8}$. Then,

$$^-5 + \frac{5}{8} = {}^-4\frac{3}{8} \quad \text{as before.}$$

Multiplication of fractions

Using the following example: $3\dfrac{1}{4} \times \dfrac{5}{6}$

1. Convert each number to an improper fraction.

$$3\frac{1}{4} = \frac{(12+1)}{4} = \frac{13}{4}$$
$\dfrac{5}{6}$ is already in reduced form.

2. Reduce (cancel) common factors of the numerator and denominator if they exist.

$\dfrac{13}{4} \times \dfrac{5}{6}$ No common factors exist.

3. Multiply the numerators by each other and the denominators by each other.

$$\frac{13}{4} \times \frac{5}{6} = \frac{65}{24}$$

4. If possible, reduce the fraction back to its lowest term.

$\dfrac{65}{24}$ Cannot be reduced further.

5. Convert the improper fraction back to a mixed fraction by using long division.

$$\frac{65}{24} = 24\overline{)65} \qquad = 2\frac{17}{24}$$
$$\underline{48}$$
$$17$$

Summary of sign changes for multiplication:

a. $(+) \times (+) = (+)$

b. $(-) \times (+) = (-)$

c. $(+) \times (-) = (-)$

d. $(-) \times (-) = (+)$

Example: $7\frac{1}{3} \times \frac{5}{11} = \frac{22}{3} \times \frac{5}{11}$ Reduce like terms (22 and 11)

$= \frac{2}{3} \times \frac{5}{1} = \frac{10}{3} = 3\frac{1}{3}$

Example: $^-6\frac{1}{4} \times \frac{5}{9} = \frac{^-25}{4} \times \frac{5}{9}$

$= \frac{^-125}{36} = ^- 3\frac{17}{36}$

Example: $\frac{^-1}{4} \times \frac{^-3}{7}$ Negative times a negative equals a positive.

$= \frac{1}{4} \times \frac{3}{7} = \frac{3}{28}$

Division of fractions:

1. Change mixed fractions to improper fractions.

2. Change the division problem to a multiplication problem by using the reciprocal of the number after the division sign.

3. Find the sign of the final product.

4. Cancel common factors if they exist between the numerator and the denominator.

5. Multiply the numerators together and the denominators together.

6. Change the improper fraction to a mixed number.

Example: $3\frac{1}{5} \div 2\frac{1}{4} = \frac{16}{5} \div \frac{9}{4}$

$= \frac{16}{5} \times \frac{4}{9}$ Reciprocal of $\frac{9}{4}$ is $\frac{4}{9}$.

$= \frac{64}{45} = 1\frac{19}{45}$

Example: $7\dfrac{3}{4} \div 11\dfrac{5}{8} = \dfrac{31}{4} \div \dfrac{93}{8}$

$= \dfrac{31}{4} \times \dfrac{8}{93}$ Reduce like terms.

$= \dfrac{1}{1} \times \dfrac{2}{3} = \dfrac{2}{3}$

Example: $\left(^-2\dfrac{1}{2}\right) \div 4\dfrac{1}{6} = \dfrac{^-5}{2} \div \dfrac{25}{6}$

$= \dfrac{^-5}{2} \times \dfrac{6}{25}$ Reduce like terms.

$= \dfrac{^-1}{1} \times \dfrac{3}{5} = \dfrac{^-3}{5}$

Example: $\left(^-5\dfrac{3}{8}\right) \div \left(\dfrac{^-7}{16}\right) = \dfrac{^-43}{8} \div \dfrac{^-7}{16}$

$= \dfrac{^-43}{8} \times \dfrac{^-16}{7}$ Reduce like terms.

$= \dfrac{43}{1} \times \dfrac{2}{7}$ Negative times a negative equals a positive.

$= \dfrac{86}{7} = 12\dfrac{2}{7}$

Skill 6.4 **Determine and perform necessary arithmetic operations to solve a practical mathematics problem (e.g., determine the total invoice cost for ordered supplies by multiplying quantity by unit price, summing all items)**

○ See Skill 6.2 and 6.3

Skill 6.5 **Solve simple algebraic problems (e.g., equations with one unknown)**

Procedure for solving algebraic equations.

Example: $3(x + 3) = {}^- 2x + 4$ Solve for x.

1) Expand to eliminate all parentheses.

$$3x + 9 = {}^- 2x + 4$$

2) Multiply each term by the LCD to eliminate all denominators.

3) Combine like terms on each side when possible.

4) Use the properties of arithmetic to put all variables on one side and all constants on the other side.

$\rightarrow 3x + 9 - 9 = {}^- 2x + 4 - 9$ (subtract nine from both sides)

$\rightarrow 3x = {}^- 2x - 5$

$\rightarrow 3x + 2x = {}^- 2x + 2x - 5$ (add 2x to both sides)

$\rightarrow 5x = {}^- 5$

$\rightarrow \dfrac{5x}{5} = \dfrac{{}^- 5}{5}$ (divide both sides by 5)

$\rightarrow x = {}^- 1$

Example: Solve $3(2x+5)-4x=5(x+9)$

$$6x+15-4x=5x+45$$

$$2x+15=5x+45$$

$$^-3x+15=45$$

$$^-3x=30$$

$$x=^-10$$

Example: Mark and Mike are twins. Three times Mark's age plus four equals four times Mike's age minus 14. How old are the boys?

Since the boys are twins, their ages are the same. "Translate" the English into Algebra. Let x = their age.

$3x + 4 = 4x - 14$

$18 = x$

The boys are each 18 years old.

Example: The YMCA wants to sell raffle tickets to raise $32,000. If they must pay $7,250 in expenses and prizes out of the money collected from the tickets, how many tickets worth $25 each must they sell?

Let x = number of tickets sold
Then $25x$ = total money collected for x tickets

Total money minus expenses is greater than $32,000.

25x – 7250 = 32,000
25x = 39350
x = 1570

If they sell 1,570 tickets, they will raise $32,000.

Example: The Simpsons went out for dinner. All 4 of them ordered the aardvark steak dinner. Bert paid for the 4 meals and included a tip of $12 for a total of $84.60. How much was an aardvark steak dinner?

Let x = the price of one aardvark dinner.
So $4x$ = the price of 4 aardvark dinners.

$$4x+12=84.60$$

$$4x=72.60$$

$$x=\$18.50 \text{ for each dinner.}$$

Skill 6.6   **Determine whether enough information is given to solve a problem**

Some problems do not contain enough information to solve them.

For example:

During one semester, a college student used 70 gallons of gas driving back and forth to visit her family. The total cost of gas was $225. What was the average number of gallons of gas used per trip?

We cannot answer this question because we do not know the number of trips the student made.

Example: A fish is 30 inches long. The head is as long as the tail. If the head was twice as long and the tail was its present length, the body would be 18 inches long. How long is the body?

Partial solution: Let x represent the head.

$$2x + x + 18 = 30$$
$$3x = 12$$
$$x = 4$$

We now create an equation to solve for the body of the fish with y representing the body.

$$x + x + y = 30$$
$$2x + y = 30$$
Substitute 4 for x.
$$2(4) + y = 30$$
$$8 + y = 30$$
$$y = 22$$

In this example, we are able to substitute the partial solution to solve for the variable in the problem's actual question.

Example: How many squares must we add to a 10-by-10 square to create an 11-by-11 square?

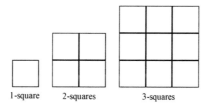

1-square   2-squares   3-squares

Partial solution: We determine that a 3-by-3 square has 5 more squares than a 2-by-2 square, which has 3 more squares than 1 square.

By examining the pattern, we see that we can answer the question by adding the dimension of the previous square (in this case, 10) to the dimension of the current square (in this case, 11) to answer the question. We must add twenty-one squares to a 10-by-10 square to create an 11-by-11 square.

Skill 6.7   Recognize alternative mathematical methods of solving a problem

Successful math teachers introduce their students to multiple problem solving strategies and create a classroom environment that encourages free thought and experimentation. Teachers can promote problem solving by allowing multiple attempts at problems, giving credit for reworking test or homework problems, and encouraging the sharing of ideas through class discussion. There are several specific problem solving skills with which teachers should be familiar.

The **guess-and-check** strategy calls for students to make an initial guess at the solution, check the answer, and use the outcome of to guide the next guess. With each successive guess, the student should get closer to the correct answer. Constructing a table from the guesses can help organize the data.

Example: There are 100 coins in a jar. 10 are dimes and the rest are pennies and nickels. There are twice as many pennies as nickels. How many pennies and nickels are in the jar?

There are 90 total nickels and pennies in the jar (100 coins – 10 dimes).

There are twice as many pennies as nickels. Make guesses that fulfill the criteria and adjust based on the answer found. Continue until we find the correct answer, 60 pennies and 30 nickels.

Number of Pennies	Number of Nickels	Total Number of Pennies and Nickels
40	20	60
80	40	120
70	35	105
60	30	90

When solving a problem where the final result and the steps to reach the result are given, **work backwards** to determine what the starting point must have been.

Example: John subtracted seven from his age, and divided the result by 3. The final result was 4. What is John's age?

Work backward by reversing the operations.
$4 \times 3 = 12$;
$12 + 7 = 19$
John is 19 years old.

Drawing pictures or diagrams can sometimes help to make relationships in a problem clearer.

For example: In a women's marathon, the first five finishers in some order were Freida, Polly, Christa, Betty, and Dora. Freida finished seven seconds before Christa. Polly finished six seconds after Betty. Dora finished eight seconds after Betty. Christa finished two seconds before Polly. In what order did the women finish the race?

Drawing a picture or diagram will help us see the answer easily.

From the diagram, we can see that the women finished in the following order: 1st – Freida, 2nd – Betty, 3rd – Christa, 4th – Polly, and 5th – Dora.

Sometimes, using a model is the best way to see the solution to a problem, as in the case of fraction multiplication.

For example: Model $\dfrac{5}{6} \times \dfrac{2}{3}$.

Draw a rectangle. Divide it vertically into 6 equal sections (the denominator of the first number).

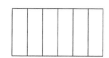

Divide the rectangle horizontally into 3 equal sections (the denominator of the second number).

Color in a number of vertical strips equal to the numerator of the first number.

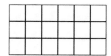

Use a different color to shade a number of horizontal strips equal to the numerator of the second number.

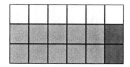

The area where the colors overlap is the product of the two fractions, $\dfrac{10}{18}$.

COMPETENCY 7.0   NUMERICAL & GRAPHIC RELATIONSHIPS

Skill 7.1   Recognize relationships in numerical data (e.g., compute a percentage change from one year to the next)

We use tables, graphs, and rules to represent relationships between two quantities. In this example, the rule $y = 9x$ describes the relationship between the total amount earned, y, and the total amount of $9 sunglasses sold, x.

Number of Sunglasses Sold	1	5	10	15
Total Dollars Earned	9	45	90	135

Each *(x,y)* relationship between a pair of values is a coordinate pair and can be plotted on a graph. The coordinate pairs *(1,9), (5,45), (10,90),* and *(15,135)* are plotted on the graph below.

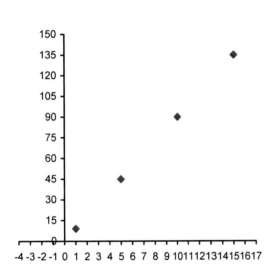

The graph (left) shows a linear relationship. A linear relationship is one in which two quantities are proportional to each other. Doubling *x* also doubles *y*. On a graph, a straight line depicts a linear relationship.

We can analyze the function or relationship between two quantities to determine how one quantity depends on the other. For example, the function below shows a relationship between *y* and *x*: $y = 2x+1$.

We can analyze the relationship between two or more variables using a table, graph, written description, or symbolic rule. The function, $y = 2x+1$, is a symbolic rule. The table (below) is another representation of the same relationship.

x	0	2	3	6	9
y	1	5	7	13	19

Alternatively, we could describe the relationship in words by saying the value of y is equal to two times the value of x, plus one. Finally, we could show the relationship on a graph by plotting given points such as the ones shown in the table above.

Another way to describe a function is as a process in which one or more numbers are input into an imaginary machine that produces another number as the output. If 5 is the input, x, and the process is x + 1, the output, y, will equal 6.

In real situations, we can describe relationships mathematically. We can use the function $y = x + 1$ to represent the idea that people age one year on their birthday. To describe the relationship in which a person's monthly medical costs are 6 times a person's age, we could write $y = 6x$. Where y is the monthly medical costs and x is the person's age. We could predict the monthly cost of medical care using this function. A 20 year-old person would spend $120 per month (120 = 20*6). An 80 year-old person would spend $480 per month (480 = 80*6). Thus, one could analyze the relationship to say: as you get older, medical costs increase $6.00 each year.

Skill 7.2   Recognize the position of numbers in relation to each other (e.g., 1/3 is between 1/4 and 1/2; -7< -4)

See also 7.3

Whole Number Place Value

Consider the number 792. We can assign a place value to each digit.

Reading from left to right, the first digit (7) represents the hundreds place. The hundreds place tells us how many sets of one hundred the number contains. Thus, there are 7 sets of one hundred in the number 792.

The second digit (9) represents the tens place. The tens place tells us how many sets of ten the number contains. Thus, there are 9 sets of ten in the number 792.

The last digit (2) represents the ones place. The ones place tells us how many ones the number contains. Thus, there are 2 sets of one in the number 792.

Therefore, there are 7 sets of 100, plus 9 sets of 10, plus 2 ones in the number 792.

Decimal Place Value

More complex numbers have additional place values to both the left and right of the decimal point. Consider the number 374.8.

Reading from left to right, the first digit (3) is in the hundreds place and tells us the number contains 3 sets of one hundred.

The second digit (7) is in the tens place and tells us the number contains 7 sets of ten.

The third digit (4) is in the ones place and tells us the number contains 4 ones.

Finally, the number after the decimal (8) is in the tenths place and tells us the number contains 8 tenths.

Place Value for Older Students

Each digit to the left of the decimal point increases progressively in powers of ten. Each digit to the right of the decimal point decreases progressively in powers of ten.

Example: 12345.6789 occupies the following powers of ten positions:

10^4	10^3	10^2	10^1	10^0	0	10^{-1}	10^{-2}	10^{-3}	10^{-4}
1	2	3	4	5	.	6	7	8	9

Names of power-of-ten positions:

10^0 = ones (note that any non-zero base raised to power zero is 1).

10^1 = tens   (number 1 and 1 zero or 10)

10^2 = hundreds   (number 1 and 2 zeros or 100)

10^3 = thousand   (number 1 and 3 zeros or 1000)

10^4 = ten thousand   (number 1 and 4 zeros or 10000)

$10^{-1} = \dfrac{1}{10^1} = \dfrac{1}{10}$ = tenth   (1st digit after decimal point or 0.1)

$10^{-2} = \dfrac{1}{10^2} = \dfrac{1}{100}$ = hundredth   (2nd digit after decimal point or 0.01)

$10^{-3} = \dfrac{1}{10^3} = \dfrac{1}{1000}$ = thousandth   (3rd digit after decimal point or 0.001)

$10^{-4} = \dfrac{1}{10^4} = \dfrac{1}{10000}$ = ten thousandth   (4th digit after decimal point or 0.0001)

Example: Write 73169.00537 in expanded form.

We start by listing all the powers of ten positions.

10^4 10^3 10^2 10^1 10^0 . 10^{-1} 10^{-2} 10^{-3} 10^{-4} 10^{-5}

Multiply each digit by its power of ten. Add all the results.

Thus $73169.00537 = (7 \times 10^4) + (3 \times 10^3) + (1 \times 10^2) + (6 \times 10^1)$
$+ (9 \times 10^0) + (0 \times 10^{-1}) + (0 \times 10^{-2}) + (5 \times 10^{-3})$
$+ (3 \times 10^{-4}) + (7 \times 10^{-5})$

Example: Determine the place value associated with the underlined digit in 3.16<u>9</u>5.

10^0 . 10^{-1} 10^{-2} 10^{-3} 10^{-4}
3   .   1   6   9   5

The place value for the digit 9 is 10^{-3} or $\dfrac{1}{1000}$.

Example: Write 21×10^3 in standard form.

$= 21 \times 1000 = 21{,}000$

Example: Write 739×10^{-4} in standard form.

$= 739 \times \dfrac{1}{10000} = \dfrac{739}{10000} = 0.0739$

Skill 7.3 **Use the relations less than, greater than, or equal to, and their associated symbols to express a numerical relationship**

Symbol for inequality: In the symbol > (greater than) or < (less than), the big open side of the symbol always faces the larger of the two numbers and the point of the symbol always faces the smaller number.

Example: Compare 15 and 20 on the number line.

Since 20 is further away from the zero than 15 is, 20 is greater than 15, or $20 > 15$.

Example: Compare $\dfrac{3}{7}$ and $\dfrac{5}{10}$.

To compare fractions, they should have the same least common denominator (LCD). The LCD in this example is 70.

$$\frac{3}{7} = \frac{3 \times 10}{7 \times 10} = \frac{30}{70} \qquad\qquad \frac{5}{10} = \frac{5 \times 7}{10 \times 7} = \frac{35}{70}$$

Since the denominators are equal, compare only the denominators. $30 < 35$, so:

$$\frac{3}{7} < \frac{5}{10}$$

Skill 7.4   Identify numbers, formulas, and mathematical expressions that are mathematically equivalent (e.g., 2/4 = 1/2, 1/4 = 25%)

Identifying mathematical equivalency requires the ability to convert between different forms of numbers and expressions. Decimals, percents, and fractions are three common forms that you should be able to convert between.

We can convert **decimals** to **percents** by multiplying by 100, or merely moving the decimal point two places to the right. We can convert **percents** to **decimals** by dividing by 100, or moving the decimal point two places to the left.

Examples: $0.375 = 37.5\%$
$0.7 = 70\%$
$0.04 = 4\%$
$3.15 = 315\%$
$84\% = 0.84$
$3\% = 0.03$
$60\% = 0.6$
$110\% = 1.1$
$\frac{1}{2}\% = 0.5\% = 0.005$

We can convert **percents** to **fractions** by placing the percentage value over 100 and reducing to simplest terms. We can convert decimals to fractions by multiplying by some fractional representation of 1.

Example: Convert 0.056 to a fraction.

Multiplying 0.056 by $\dfrac{1000}{1000}$ to get rid of the decimal point:

$$0.056 \times \frac{1000}{1000} = \frac{56}{1000} = \frac{7}{125}$$

Example: Find 23% of 1000.

$$= \frac{23}{100} \times \frac{1000}{1} = 23 \times 10 = 230$$

Example: Convert 6.25% to a decimal and to a fraction.

$$6.25\% = 0.0625 = 0.0625 \times \frac{10000}{10000} = \frac{625}{10000} = \frac{1}{16}$$

An example of a type of problem involving fractions is the conversion of recipes. For example, if a recipe serves 8 people and we want to make enough to serve only 4, we must determine how much of each ingredient we should use. The conversion factor, the number we multiply each ingredient by, is:

$$\text{Conversion Factor} = \frac{\text{Number of Servings Needed}}{\text{Number of Servings in Recipe}}$$

Example: Consider the following recipe.

3 cups flour
½ tsp. baking powder
2/3 cups butter
2 cups sugar
2 eggs

If the above recipe serves 8, how much of each ingredient do we need to serve only 4 people?

First, determine the conversion factor.

$$\text{Conversion Factor} = \frac{4}{8} = \frac{1}{2}$$

Next, multiply each ingredient by the conversion factor.

3 x ½ =	1 ½ cups flour
½ x ½ =	¼ tsp. baking powder
2/3 x ½ = 2/6 =	1/3 cups butter
2 x ½ =	1 cup sugar
2 x ½ =	1 egg

Skill 7.5   Understand and use rounding rules when solving problems

To estimate measurement of familiar objects, it is first necessary to determine the units to use.

Examples:
Length
1. The coastline of California
2. The width of a ribbon
3. The thickness of a book
4. The depth of water in a pool

Weight or mass
1. A bag of sugar
2. A school bus
3. A dime

Capacity or volume
1. Paint in a paint can
2. Glass of milk

Money
1. Cost of a house
2. Cost of a cup of coffee
3. Exchange rate

Perimeter
1. The edge of a backyard
2. The edge of a football field

Area
1. The size of a carpet
2. The size of a state

Example: Estimate the measurements of the following objects:

Length of a dollar bill	6 inches
Weight of a baseball	1 pound
Distance from New York to Florida	1100 km
Volume of water to fill a medicine dropper	1 milliliter
Length of a desk	2 meters
Temperature of water in a swimming pool	80° F

Depending on the degree of accuracy needed, we can measure an object with different units. For example, a pencil may be 6 inches to the nearest inch or 6 3/8 inches to the nearest eighth of an inch. Similarly, it might be 15 cm to the nearest centimeter or 154 mm to the nearest millimeter.

Given a set of objects and their measurements, the use of rounding procedures is helpful when attempting to round to the nearest given unit. When rounding to a given place value, it is necessary to look at the number in the next smaller place. If this number is 5 or more, we increase the number in the place we are rounding and change all numbers to the right to zero. If the number is less than 5, the we leave the number in the place we are rounding the same and change all numbers to the right to zero.

One method of rounding measurements can require an additional step. First, we must convert the measurement to a decimal number. Then, we apply the rules for rounding.

Example: Round the measurements to the given units.

MEASUREMENT	ROUND TO NEAREST	ANSWER
1 foot 7 inches	foot	2 ft
5 pound 6 ounces	pound	5 pounds
5 9/16 inches	inch	6 inches

Convert each measurement to a decimal number, then apply the rules for rounding.

1 foot 7 inches = $1\frac{7}{12}$ ft = 1.58333 ft, round up to 2 ft

5 pounds 6 ounces = $5\frac{6}{16}$ pounds = 5.375 pound, round to 5 pounds

$5\frac{9}{16}$ inches = 5.5625 inches, round up to 6 inches

Rounding numbers is a form of estimation that is very useful in many mathematical operations. For example, when estimating the sum of two three-digit numbers, it is helpful to round the two numbers to the nearest hundred prior to addition. We can round numbers to any place value.

Rounding whole numbers

To round whole numbers, you first find the place value you want to round to (the rounding digit) and look at the digit directly to the right. If the digit is less than five, do not change the rounding digit and replace all numbers after the rounding digit with zeroes. If the digit is greater than or equal to five, increase the rounding digit by one and replace all numbers after the rounding digit with zeroes.

Example: Round 517 to the nearest ten.

1 is the rounding digit because it occupies the tens place.

517 rounded to the nearest ten = 520; because 7 > 5 we add one to the rounding digit.

Example: Round 15,449 to the nearest hundred.

The first 4 is the rounding digit because it occupies the hundreds place.

15,449 rounded to the nearest hundred = 15,400, because 4 < 5 we do not add to the rounding digit.

Rounding decimals

Rounding decimals is identical to rounding whole numbers except that you simply drop all the digits to the right of the rounding digit.

Example: Round 417.3621 to the nearest tenth.

3 is the rounding digit because it occupies the tenth place.

417.3621 rounded to the nearest tenth = 417.4; because 6 > 5 we add one to the rounding digit.

Skill 7.6   Understand and apply the meaning of logical connectives (e.g., and, or, if-then) and quantifiers (e.g., some, all, none)

A simple statement represents a simple idea that can be described as either "true" or "false," but not both. We represent simple statements with small letters of the alphabet.

Example: "Today is Monday." This is a simple statement since we can determine if the statement is true or false. We can write p = "Today is Monday."

Example: "John, please be quiet." This is not considered a simple statement in our study of logic, since we cannot assign a truth value to it.

Simple statements joined together by **connectives** ("and," "or," "not," "if then," and "if and only if") result in compound statements. Note that compound statements can also contain "but," "however," or "nevertheless." We can assign a truth value to a compound statement.

Conditional statements are frequently written in "if-then" form. The "if" clause of the conditional is the **hypothesis**, and the "then" clause is the **conclusion**. In a proof, the hypothesis is the information that we assume to be true, while the conclusion is what is what we prove to be true. A conditional takes the form: **If p, then q** where p is the hypothesis and q is the conclusion.

$p \rightarrow q$ is read "if p, then q."
~ (statement) is read "it is not true that (statement)."

Quantifiers are words describing a quantity. These include words like "all," "none" (or "no"), and "some."

Negation of a Statement- If a statement is true, then its negation must be false (and vice versa).

A Summary of Negation Rules:

statement	negation
(1) q	(1) not q
(2) not q	(2) q
(3) π and s	(3) (not π) or (not s)
(4) π or s	(4) (not π) and (not s)
(5) if p, then q	(5) (p) and (not q)

Example: Select the statement that is the negation of "Some winter nights are not cold."

A. All winter nights are not cold.
B. Some winter nights are cold.
C. All winter nights are cold.
D. No winter nights are cold.

Negation of "some are" is "none are." So the negation statement is "No winter nights are cold." So the answer is D.

Example: Select the statement that is the negation of "If it rains, then the beach party will not be held."

A. If it does not rain, then the beach party will be held.
B. If the beach party is held, then it will not rain.
C. It does not rain and the beach party will be held.
D. It rains and the beach party will be held.

Negation of "if p, then q" is "p and (not q)." So the negation of the given statement is "It rains and the beach party will be held." So select D.

Example: Select the negation of the statement "If they get elected, then all politicians go back on election promises."

A. If they get elected, then many politicians go back on election promises.
B. They get elected and some politicians go back on election promises.
C. If they do not get elected, some politicians do not go back on election promises.
D. None of the above statements is the negation of the given statement.

Identify the key words of "if... then" and "all... go back." The negation of the given statement is "they get elected and none of the politicians go back on election promises." So select response D, since statements A, B, and C are not the negations.

Example: Select the statement that is the negation of "The sun is shining bright <u>and</u> I feel great."

A. If the sun is not shining bright. I do not feel great.
B. The sun is not shining bright and I do not feel great.
C. The sun is not shining bright or I do not feel great.
D. The sun is shining bright and I do not feel great.

The negation of "r and s" is "(not r) or (not s)." So the negation of the given statement is "The sun is <u>not</u> shining bright <u>or</u> I do not feel great." (C).

We can diagram conditional statements using a **Venn diagram**. Venn diagrams consist of one circle drawn inside another circle. The inner circle represents the hypothesis and the outer circle represents the conclusion. If the hypothesis is taken to be true, then you are located inside the inner circle. If you are located in the inner circle then you are also inside the outer circle, so that proves the conclusion is true.

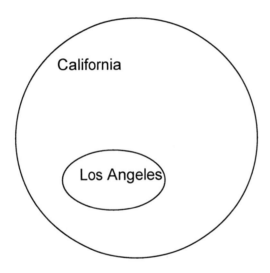

Example: If you are in Los Angeles, then you are in California.

In this statement "you are in Los Angeles" is the hypothesis.
In this statement "you are in California" is the conclusion.

Skill 7.7   Identify or specify a missing entry from a table of data (e.g., subtotal)

Example:
Corporate Earnings for ACME Company

	Division A	Division B	Division C
January	10,000	30,000	20,000
February	15,000	25,000	15,000
March	25,000	20,000	25,000
1st quarter	50,000	75,000	60,000
April	20,000	35,000	20,000
May	10,000	10,000	30,000
June	20,000	15,000	25,000
2nd quarter	50,000	60,000	75,000
July	15,000	25,000	20,000
August	25,000	20,000	35,000
September	20,000	10,000	10,000
3rd quarter	60,000	55,000	65,000
October	30,000	20,000	15,000
November	25,000	30,000	35,000
December	20,000	10,000	20,000
Total	235,000	250,000	270,000

In this example, the table shows monthly earnings and quarterly subtotals. You should check the columnar totals by first checking each subtotal (quarter). When you do this, you see that October-November do not add up to the total, which tells you something is missing (the subtotal for the 4th quarter).

If you check the total by adding the subtotals (quarters), you would also see that you are missing a 4th quarter subtotal. If you were not looking at the line description and just added the next-to-last figure to the other subtotals, assuming that it was a subtotal, you would also see that you are missing something because the subtotals would not add up to the total.

Skill 7.8   Use numerical information contained in tables, spreadsheets, and various kinds of graphs (e.g., bar, line, circle) to solve mathematics problems

To make a **bar graph** or a **pictograph**, determine the scale to use for the graph. Then determine the length of each bar on the graph or determine the number of pictures needed to represent each item of information. Be sure to include an explanation of the scale in the legend.

Example: A class had the following grades:
4 A's, 9 B's, 8 C's, 1 D, 3 F's.
Graph these on a bar graph and a pictograph.

Pictograph

Grade	Number of Students
A	☺☺☺☺
B	☺☺☺☺☺☺☺☺☺
C	☺☺☺☺☺☺☺☺
D	☺
F	☺☺☺

Bar graph

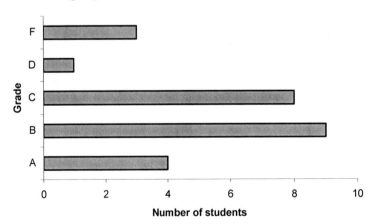

To make a **line graph**, determine appropriate scales for both the vertical and horizontal axes (based on the information). Describe what each axis represents and mark the scale periodically on each axis. Graph the individual points of the graph and connect the points on the graph from left to right.

Example: Graph the following information using a line graph.

The number of National Merit finalists per school per year

	90-91	91-92	92-93	93-94	94-95	95-96
Central	3	5	1	4	6	8
Wilson	4	2	3	2	3	2

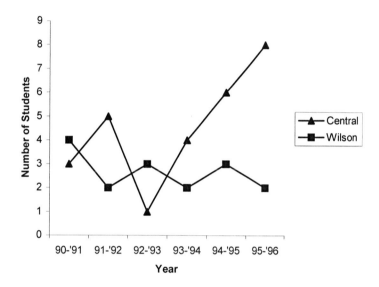

To make a **circle graph**, total all the information. Determine the central angle to use for each sector of the graph using the following formula:

$$\frac{\text{information}}{\text{total information}} \times 360° = \text{degrees in central } \angle$$

Lay out the central angles to match these sizes, label each section, and include its percent.

Example: Graph this information on a circle graph:

Monthly expenses:

Rent, $400
Food, $150
Utilities, $75
Clothes, $75
Church, $100
Misc., $200

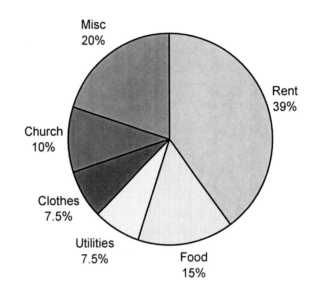

Histograms summarize information from large sets of data that can be naturally grouped into intervals. The vertical axis indicates **frequency** (the number of times any particular data value occurs), and the horizontal axis indicates data values or ranges of data values. The number of data values in any interval is the **frequency of the interval**.

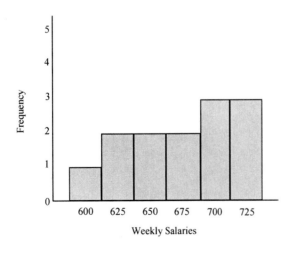

Sample Test

Mathematics

1. **What unit of measurement would describe the spread of a forest fire in a unit time?**
(Average Rigor) (Skill 4.1)

   A. 10 square yards per second

   B. 10 yards per minute

   C. 10 feet per hour

   D. 10 cubic feet per hour

2. **What unit of measurement could we use to report the distance traveled walking around a track?**
(Easy) (Skill 4.1)

   A. degrees

   B. square meters

   C. kilometers

   D. cubic feet

3. **What is the area of a square whose side is 13 feet?**
(Average Rigor) (Skill 4.2)

   A. 169 feet

   B. 169 square feet

   C. 52 feet

   D. 52 square feet

4. **What is the area of this triangle?**

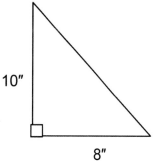

10″

8″

(Rigorous) (Skill 4.2)

   A. 80 square inches

   B. 20 square inches

   C. 40 square inches

   D. 30 square inches

5. **The trunk of a tree has a 2.1 meter radius. What is its circumference?**
(Rigorous) (Skill 4.2)

   A. 2.1π square meters

   B. 4.2π meters

   C. 2.1π meters

   D. 4.2π square meters

6. The owner of a rectangular piece of land 40 yards in length and 30 yards in width wants to divide it into two parts. She plans to join two opposite corners with a fence as shown in the diagram below. The cost of the fence will be approximately $25 per linear foot. What is the estimated cost for the fence needed by the owner?

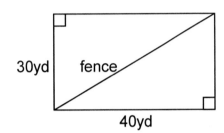

(Rigorous) (Skill 4.2)

A. $1,250

B. $62,500

C. $5,250

D. $3,750

7. Carla has three subjects for homework. She has 10 math problems which should take 5 minutes each, a paragraph which should take 45 minutes to write, and a worksheet packet which will take 1 hour and 50 minutes. How much time does Carla estimate she will spend on homework?
(Average Rigor) (Skill 4.3)

A. 3 hours

B. 4 hours

C. 2 hours

D. Less than an hour

8. Solve for X.
⁻3 + ⁻32 + 23 = X
(Average Rigor) (Skill 6.2)

A. 12

B. ⁻12

C. 58

D. 85

9. A car gets 25.36 miles per gallon. The car has been driven 83,310 miles. What is a reasonable estimate for the number of gallons of gas used?
(Average Rigor) (Skill 4.4)

A. 2,087 gallons

B. 3,000 gallons

C. 1,800 gallons

D. 164 gallons

10. In a sample of 40 full-time employees at a particular company, 35 were also holding down a part-time job requiring at least 10 hours/week. If this proportion holds for the entire company of 25000 employees, how many full-time employees at this company are actually holding down a part-time job of at least 10 hours per week.
(Rigorous) (Skill 5.1)

A. 714

B. 625

C. 21,875

D. 28,571

11. What is the mode of the data in the following sample?

9, 10, 11, 9, 10, 11, 9, 13
(Average Rigor) (Skill 5.1)

A. 9

B. 9.5

C. 10

D. 11

12. What is the mean of the data in the following sample?

9, 10, 11, 9, 10, 11, 9, 11
(Average Rigor) (Skill 5.1)

A. 8

B. 9

C. 10

D. 11

13. Corporate salaries are listed for several employees. Which is the best measure of central tendency?

$24,000 $24,000 $26,000
$28,000 $30,000 $120,000

(Rigorous) (Skill 5.1)

A. Mean

B. Median

C. Mode

D. No difference

14. Mary did comparison shopping on her favorite brand of coffee. Over half of the stores priced the coffee at $1.70. Most of the remaining stores priced the coffee at $1.80, except for a few who charged $1.90. Which of the following statements is true about the distribution of prices?
(Rigorous) (Skill 5.1)

A. The mean and the mode are the same.

B. The mean is greater than the mode.

C. The mean is less than the mode.

D. The mean is less than the median.

15. What is the probability of drawing 2 consecutive aces from a standard deck of cards?
(Rigorous) (Skill 5.2)

A. $\dfrac{3}{51}$

B. $\dfrac{1}{221}$

C. $\dfrac{2}{104}$

D. $\dfrac{2}{52}$

16. Given a drawer with 5 black socks, 3 blue socks, and 2 red socks, what is the probability that you will draw two black socks in two draws in a dark room?
(Rigorous) (Skill 5.2)

A. 2/9

B. ¼

C. 17/18

D. 1/18

17. Two mathematics classes have a total of 410 students. The 8 am class has 40 more than the 10 am class. How many students are in the 10 am class?
(Rigorous) (Skill 6.1)

   A.   123.3

   B.   370

   C.   185

   D.   330

18. $\left(\dfrac{^-4}{9}\right)+\left(\dfrac{^-7}{10}\right)=$
(Average Rigor) (Skill 6.3)

   A. $\dfrac{23}{90}$

   B. $\dfrac{^-23}{90}$

   C. $\dfrac{103}{90}$

   D. $\dfrac{^-103}{90}$

19. $(5.6)\times\left(^-0.11\right)=$
(Average Rigor) (Skill 6.3)

   A. $^-0.616$

   B.   0.616

   C. $^-6.110$

   D.   6.110

20. $4\dfrac{2}{9}$ x $\dfrac{7}{10}$
(Rigorous) (Skill 6.3)

   A. $4\dfrac{9}{10}$

   B. $\dfrac{266}{90}$

   C. $2\dfrac{43}{45}$

   D. $2\dfrac{6}{20}$

21. 0.74 =
(Easy) (Skill 6.3)

   A. $\dfrac{74}{100}$

   B.   7.4%

   C. $\dfrac{33}{50}$

   D. $\dfrac{74}{10}$

22. $\dfrac{7}{9} + \dfrac{1}{3} \div \dfrac{2}{3} =$

(Average Rigor) (Skill 6.3)

A. $\dfrac{5}{3}$

B. $\dfrac{3}{2}$

C. 2

D. $\dfrac{23}{18}$

23. A sofa sells for $520. If the retailer makes a 30% profit, what was the wholesale price?
(Average Rigor) (Skill 6.3)

A. $400

B. $676

C. $490

D. $364

24. $(^-2.1 \times 10^4)(4.2 \times 10^{-5}) =$
(Rigorous) (Skill 6.3)

A. 8.82

B. -8.82

C. -0.882

D. 0.882

25. 303 is what percent of 600?
(Easy) (Skill 6.3)

A. 0.505%

B. 5.05%

C. 505%

D. 50.5%

26. An item that sells for $375 is put on sale at $120. What is the percent of decrease?
(Average Rigor) (Skill 6.4)

A. 25%

B. 28%

C. 68%

D. 34%

27. A restaurant employs 465 people. There are 280 waiters and 185 cooks. If 168 waiters and 85 cooks receive pay raises, what percent of the waiters received a pay raise?
(Average Rigor) (Skill 6.4)

A. 36.13%

B. 60%

C. 60.22%

D. 40%

28. The price of gas is $3.27 per gallon. Your tank holds 15 gallons of fuel. You are using two tanks a week. Approximately how much will you save weekly if the price of gas goes down to $2.30 per gallon?
(Average Rigor) (Skill 6.4)

A. $26.00

B. $29.00

C. $15.00

D. $17.00

29. A boat travels 30 miles upstream in three hours. It makes the return trip in one and a half hours. What is the speed of the boat in still water?
(Average Rigor) (Skill 6.4)

A. 10 mph

B. 15 mph

C. 20 mph

D. 30 mph

30. Given the formula *d = rt*, (where *d* = distance, *r* = rate, and *t* = time), calculate the time required for a vehicle to travel 585 miles at a rate of 65 miles per hour.
(Average Rigor) (Skill 6.4)

A. 8.5 hours

B. 6.5 hours

C. 9.5 hours

D. 9 hours

31. Which of the equations below has $x = \frac{1}{6}$ as a solution?

i. $6x \le 4x^2 + 2$
ii. $10x + 1 = 3(4x - 3)$
iii. $|x - 1| = x$
(Rigorous) (Skill 6.5)

A. i, ii, and iii

B. i and iii only

C. i only

D. iii only

32. The figure below shows a running track and the shape of an inscribed rectangle with semicircles at each end.

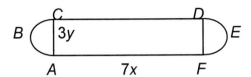

Calculate the distance around the track.
(Rigorous) (Skill 4.2)

A. $6\pi y + 14x$

B. $3\pi y + 7x$

C. $6\pi y + 7x$

D. $3\pi y + 14x$

33. Choose the expression that is *not* equivalent to 5x + 3y + 15z:
(Average Rigor) (Skill 6.5)

A. 5(x + 3z) + 3y

B. 3(x + y + 5z)

C. 3y + 5(x + 3z)

D. 5x + 3(y + 5z)

34. Choose the equation that is equivalent to the following:

$$\frac{3x}{5} - 5 = 5x$$

(Rigorous) (Skill 6.5)

A. $3x - 25 = 25x$

B. $x - \frac{25}{3} = 25x$

C. $6x - 50 = 75x$

D. $x + 25 = 25x$

35. If $4x - (3 - x) = 7(x - 3) + 10$, then
(Rigorous) (Skill 6.5)

A. $x = 8$

B. $x = -8$

C. $x = 4$

D. $x = -4$

36. Solve for x.
$$3x - \frac{2}{3} = \frac{5x}{2} + 2$$
(Rigorous) (Skill 6.5)

A. $5\frac{1}{3}$

B. $\frac{17}{3}$

C. 2

D. $\frac{16}{2}$

37. A family spends $150 a week for groceries. How much money is left at the end of the month?
(Average Rigor) (Skill 6.6)

A. $600

B. $150

C. $12

D. Not enough information

38. Sara travels 39 miles to class, 25 miles to work, and 14 miles to see her friend. How much does she spend in gas? Explain the operation needed for this problem.
(Average Rigor) (Skill 6.6)

A. Add 39 + 25 + 14

B. Mulitply the numbers by 3

C. Not enough information is given

D. Add the numbers, then mulitply by 5

39. The teacher is introducing the concept of multiplication to her third grade students. What is another way she might write 4 x 5?
(Easy) (Skill 6.7)

A. 4 + 5

B. 5 + 4

C. 4 + 4 + 4 + 4 + 4

D. 5 + 5 + 5 + 5 + 5

40. What is the equation that expresses the relationship between x and y in the table below?

x	y
-2	4
-1	1
0	-2
1	-5
2	-8

(Rigorous) (Skill 7.1)

A. $y = -x - 2$

B. $y = -3x - 2$

C. $y = 3x - 2$

D. $y = \dfrac{1}{3}x - 1$

41. Given $f(x) = (x)^3 - 3(x)^2 + 5$, find $x = (-2)$.
    (Rigorous) (Skill 7.1)

    A. 15

    B. -15

    C. 25

    D. -25

42. $(^-2.1 \times 10^4)(4.2 \times 10^{^-5}) =$
    (Rigorous) (Skill 7.2)

    A. 8.82

    B. -8.82

    C. -0.882

    D. 0.882

43. $^-9\dfrac{1}{4}$ ☐ $^-8\dfrac{2}{3}$
    (Average Rigor) (Skill 7.3)

    A. =

    B. <

    C. >

    D. ≤

44. Choose the expression that is not equivalent to 5x + 3y + 15z:
    (Average Rigor) (Skill 7.4)

    A. 5(x + 3z) + 3y

    B. 3(x + y + 5z)

    C. 3y + 5(x + 3z)

    D. 5x + 3(y + 5z)

45. Round $1\dfrac{13}{16}$ of an inch to the nearest quarter of an inch.
    (Easy) (Skill 7.5)

    A. $1\dfrac{1}{4}$ inch

    B. $1\dfrac{5}{8}$ inch

    C. $1\dfrac{3}{4}$ inch

    D. 2 inches

46. **Set A, B, C, and U are related as shown in the diagram.**

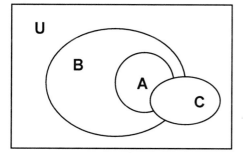

Which of the following is true, assuming not one of the six regions is empty?
(Average Rigor) (Skill 7.6)

A. Any element that is a member of set B is also a member of set A.

B. No element is a member of all three sets A, B, and C.

C. Any element that is a member of set U is also a member of set B.

D. None of the above statements is true.

47. **Select the statement that is the negation of the statement, "If the weather is cold, then the soccer game will be played."**
(Average Rigor) (Skill 7.6)

A. If the weather is not cold, then the soccer game will be played.

B. The weather is cold and the soccer game will not be played.

C. If the soccer game is played, then the weather is not cold.

D. The weather is cold and the soccer game will be played.

48. Study the information given below. If a logical conclusion is given, select that conclusion.

    Bob eats donuts or he eats yogurt. If Bob eats yogurt, then he is healthy. If Bob is healthy, then he can run the marathon. Bob does not eat yogurt.
    (Average Rigor) (Skill 7.6)

    A. Bob does not eat donuts.

    B. Bob is healthy.

    C. Bob runs the marathon.

    D. None of the above.

49. Select the statement below that is NOT logically equivalent to "If Mary works late, then Bill will prepare lunch."
    (Average Rigor) (Skill 7.6)

    A. Bill prepares lunch or Mary does not work late.

    B. If Bill does not prepare lunch, then Mary did not work late.

    C. If Bill prepares lunch, then Mary works late.

    D. Mary does not work late or Bill prepares lunch.

50. Select the rule of logical equivalence that directly (in one step) transforms the statement (i) into statement (ii),

    i. Not all the students have books.
    ii. Some students do not have books.
    (Average Rigor) (Skill 7.6)

    A. "If p, then q" is equivalent to "if not q, then b."

    B. "Not all are p" is equivalent to "some are not p."

    C. "Not q" is equivalent to "p."

    D. "All are not p" is equivalent to "none are p."

51. Given that:
    i. No athletes are weak.
    ii. All football players are athletes.

    Determine which conclusion can be logically deduced.
    (Average Rigor) (Skill 7.6)

    A. Some football players are weak.

    B. All football players are weak.

    C. No football player is weak.

    D. None of the above is true.

52. What is missing from the following graph?

Cars Sold

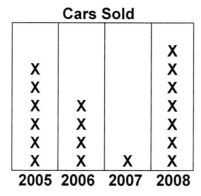

(Average Rigor) (Skill 7.7)

A. Total number of cars sold

B. Kinds of cars

C. The value of X (interval)

D. Time period covered

53. The following chart shows the yearly average number of international tourists visiting Redondo Beach for 1990-1994. How many more international tourists visited Redondo Beach in 1994 than in 1991?
    (Easy) (Skill 7.8)

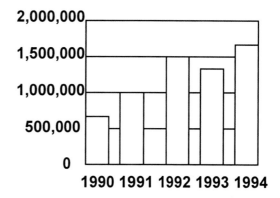

A. 100,000

B. 600,000

C. 1,600,000

D. 8,000,000

54. Consider the graph of the distribution of the length of time it took individuals to complete an employment form.

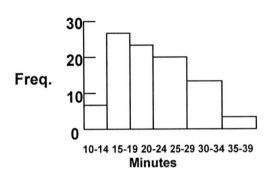

Approximately how many individuals took less than 15 minutes to complete the employment form? *(Easy) (Skill 7.8)*

A. 35

B. 28

C. 7

D. 4

55. Which statement is true about George's budget? *(Easy) (Skill 7.8)*

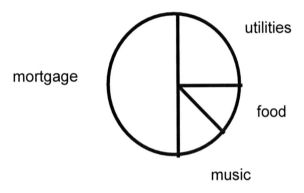

A. George spends the greatest portion of his income on food.

B. George spends twice as much on utilities as he does on his mortgage.

C. George spends twice as much on utilities as he does on food.

D. George spends the same amount on food and utilities as he does on his mortgage.

56.   The table below shows the
      distribution of majors for a
      group of college students.

Major	Proportion of students
Mathematics	0.32
Photography	0.26
Journalism	0.19
Engineering	0.21
Criminal Law	0.02

If it is known that a student chosen at random
is not majoring in mathematics or
engineering, what is the probability that a student is
majoring in journalism?
(Rigorous) (Skill 7.8)

A. 0.19

B. 0.36

C. 0.40

D. 0.81

Answer Key: Mathematics

1.	A	29.	B
2.	C	30.	D
3.	B	31.	C
4.	C	32.	D
5.	B	33.	B
6.	D	34.	A
7.	B	35.	C
8.	B	36.	A
9.	B	37.	D
10.	C	38.	C
11.	A	39.	C
12.	C	40.	B
13.	B	41.	B
14.	B	42.	C
15.	B	43.	B
16.	A	44.	B
17.	C	45.	C
18.	D	46.	D
19.	A	47.	B
20.	C	48.	D
21.	A	49.	C
22.	D	50.	B
23.	A	51.	C
24.	C	52.	C
25.	D	53.	B
26.	C	54.	C
27.	B	55.	C
28.	B	56.	C

Rigor Table: Mathematics

	Easy 20%	Average 40%	Rigorous 40%
Questions (56)	2, 21, 25, 37, 38, 39, 45, 52, 53, 54, 55	1, 3, 9, 11, 12, 18, 19, 22, 23, 26, 27, 28, 29, 30, 33, 43, 44, 46, 47, 48, 49, 50, 51	4, 5, 6, 7, 8, 10, 13, 14, 15, 16, 17, 20, 24, 31, 32, 34, 35, 36, 40, 41, 42, 56
TOTALS	11 (20%)	23 (41%)	22 (39%)

Rationales with Sample Questions: Mathematics

1. **What unit of measurement would describe the spread of a forest fire in a unit time?**
   (Average Rigor) (Skill 4.1)

   A. 10 square yards per second

   B. 10 yards per minute

   C. 10 feet per hour

   D. 10 cubic feet per hour

Answer A: 10 square yards per second

The only appropriate answer is one that describes "an area" of forest consumed per unit time. Answer A is the only answer that gives a unit of area measurement.

2. **What unit of measurement could we use to report the distance traveled walking around a track?**
   (Easy) (Skill 4.1)

   A. degrees

   B. square meters

   C. kilometers

   D. cubic feet

Answer C: kilometers

Degrees measures angles, square meters measure area, cubic feet measure volume, and kilometers measures length. Kilometers is the only reasonable answer.

3.   **What is the area of a square whose side is 13 feet?**
        (Average Rigor) (Skill 4.2)

    A. 169 feet

    B. 169 square feet

    C. 52 feet

    D. 52 square feet

Answer B: 169 square feet

Area of a square = Side x Side
Area = $13 \times 13 = 169$ square feet.
Area is measured in square feet, so the answer is B.

4.   **What is the area of this triangle?**

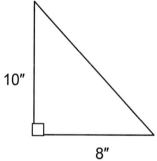

    10"

    8"

        (Rigorous) (Skill 4.2)

    A. 80 square inches

    B. 20 square inches

    C. 40 square inches

    D. 30 square inches

Answer C: 40 square inches

The area of a triangle is $\frac{1}{2}bh$. $\frac{1}{2}x8x10 = 40$ square inches (C).

5. **The trunk of a tree has a 2.1 meter radius. What is its circumference?**
    (Rigorous) (Skill 4.2)

    A. 2.1π square meters

    B. 4.2π meters

    C. $2.1\ \pi$ meters

    D. 4.2π square meters

Answer B: 4.2π meters

Circumference is $2\pi r$, where r is the radius. The circumference is $2\pi 2.1 = 4.2\pi$ meters (not square meters because not measuring area).

6.   The owner of a rectangular piece of land 40 yards in length and 30 yards in width wants to divide it into two parts. She plans to join two opposite corners with a fence as shown in the diagram below. The cost of the fence will be approximately $25 per linear foot. What is the estimated cost for the fence needed by the owner?

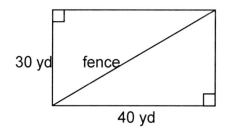

30 yd   fence

40 yd

(Rigorous) (Skill 4.2)

A. $1,250

B. $62,500

C. $5,250

D. $3,750

Answer D: $3,750

Find the length of the diagonal by using the Pythagorean theorem. Let x be the length of the diagonal.

$$30^2 + 40^2 = x^2 \rightarrow 900 + 1600 = x^2$$
$$2500 = x^2 \rightarrow \sqrt{2500} = \sqrt{x^2}$$

$$x = 50 \text{ yards}$$

Convert to feet. $\dfrac{50 \text{ yards}}{x \text{ feet}} = \dfrac{1 \text{ yard}}{3 \text{ feet}} \rightarrow 150 \text{ feet}$

It costs $25 per linear foot, so the cost is (150 ft)($25) = $3750 (D).

7.   **Carla has three subjects for homework. She has 10 math problems which should take 5 minutes each, a paragraph which should take 45 minutes to write, and a worksheet packet which will take 1 hour and 50 minutes. How much time does Carla estimate she will spend on homework?**
(Rigorous) (Skill 4.3)

A. 3 hours

B. 4 hours

C. 2 hours

D. Less than an hour

Answer B: 4 hours

10 math problems at 5 minutes each will be close to one hour. 45 minutes to write is also close to one hour. The hour and 50 minutes on the packet is almost two hours. The estimated work time is 4 hours (B).

8.   **Solve for X.**
$^-3 + {}^-32 + 23 = X$
(Rigorous) (Skill 6.2)

A. 12

B. $^-12$

C. 58

D. 85

Answer B: $^-12$

Adding two negative number results in a negative number, so $^-3 + {}^-32 = {}^-35$. Then add 23. The answer is $^-12$ (B).

9.   A car gets 25.36 miles per gallon. The car has been driven 83,310 miles. What is a reasonable estimate for the number of gallons of gas used?
       (Average Rigor) (Skill 4.4)

       A. 2,087 gallons

       B. 3,000 gallons

       C. 1,800 gallons

       D. 164 gallons

Answer B: 3,000 gallons

Divide the number of miles by the miles per gallon to determine the approximate number of gallons of gas used. $\frac{83310 \text{ miles}}{25.36 \text{ miles per gallon}} = 3285$ gallons. This is approximately 3000 gallons.

10.   In a sample of 40 full-time employees at a particular company, 35 were also holding down a part-time job requiring at least 10 hours/week. If this proportion holds for the entire company of 25,000 employees, how many full-time employees at this company are actually holding down a part-time job of at least 10 hours per week.
       (Rigorous) (Skill 5.1)

       A. 714

       B. 625

       C. 21,875

       D. 28,571

Answer C: 21,875

$\frac{35}{40}$ full time employees also have part time jobs. $\frac{35}{40}$ is 0.875 or 87.5%. Using the same proportion, 87.5% of 25,000 is 21,875.

11. **What is the mode of the data in the following sample?**

9, 10, 11, 9, 10, 11, 9, 13
(Average Rigor) (Skill 5.1)

A. 9

B. 9.5

C. 10

D. 11

Answer A: 9

The mode is the number that appears most frequently. 9 appears 3 times, which is more than the other numbers.

12. **What is the mean of the data in the following sample?**

9, 10, 11, 9, 10, 11, 9, 11
(Average Rigor) (Skill 5.1)

A. 8

B. 9

C. 10

D. 11

Answer C: 10

To find the mean (average), add all the numbers. Then divide by the number of values you added.   9 + 10 + 11 + 9 + 10 + 11 + 9 + 11 = 80
$$80 \div 8 = 10$$

13. **Corporate salaries are listed for several employees. Which is the best measure of central tendency?**

$24,000 $24,000 $26,000 $28,000 $30,000 $120,000

(Rigorous) (Skill 5.1)

A. Mean

B. Median

C. Mode

D. No difference

Answer B: Median

The median provides the best measure of central tendency in this case where the mode is the lowest number and the mean would be disproportionately skewed by the outlier $120,000.

14. **Mary did comparison shopping on her favorite brand of coffee. Over half of the stores priced the coffee at $1.70. Most of the remaining stores priced the coffee at $1.80, except for a few who charged $1.90. Which of the following statements is true about the distribution of prices?**
(Rigorous) (Skill 5.1)

A. The mean and the mode are the same.

B. The mean is greater than the mode.

C. The mean is less than the mode.

D. The mean is less than the median.

Answer B: The mean is greater than the mode.

Over half the stores priced the coffee at $1.70, so this means that this is the mode. The mean would be slightly over $1.70 because other stores priced the coffee at over $1.70.

15. **What is the probability of drawing 2 consecutive aces from a standard deck of cards?**
    (Rigorous) (Skill 5.2)

    A. $\dfrac{3}{51}$

    B. $\dfrac{1}{221}$

    C. $\dfrac{2}{104}$

    D. $\dfrac{2}{52}$

Answer B: $\dfrac{1}{221}$

There are 4 aces in the 52 card deck. P(first ace) = $\dfrac{4}{52}$. P(second ace) = $\dfrac{3}{51}$.

P(first ace and second ace) = P(one ace) x P(second ace|first ace) = $\dfrac{4}{52} \times \dfrac{3}{51}$ =

$\dfrac{1}{221}$.

16. **Given a drawer with 5 black socks, 3 blue socks, and 2 red socks, what is the probability that you will draw two black socks in two draws in a dark room?**
    (Rigorous) (Skill 5.2)

    A. 2/9

    B. ¼

    C. 17/18

    D. 1/18

Answer A: 2/9

In this example of conditional probability, the probability of drawing a black sock on the first draw is 5/10. It is implied in the problem that there is no replacement, therefore the probability of obtaining a black sock in the second draw is 4/9. Multiply the two probabilities and reduce to lowest terms.

17. Two mathematics classes have a total of 410 students. The 8 am class has 40 more than the 10 am class. How many students are in the 10 am class?
(Rigorous) (Skill 6.1)

    A.   123.3

    B.   370

    C.   185

    D.   330

Answer C: 185

Let x = # of students in the 8 am class and x – 40 = # of students in the 10 am class. X + X – 40 = 410. 2X = 410 + 40. 2X = 450. X = 225. So there are 225 students in the 8 am class, and 225 – 40 = 185 in the 10 am class, which is answer C.

18. $\left(\dfrac{-4}{9}\right) + \left(\dfrac{-7}{10}\right) =$
(Average Rigor) (Skill 6.3)

    A. $\dfrac{23}{90}$

    B. $\dfrac{-23}{90}$

    C. $\dfrac{103}{90}$

    D. $\dfrac{-103}{90}$

Answer D: $\dfrac{-103}{90}$

Find the LCD of $\frac{^-4}{9}$ and $\frac{^-7}{10}$. The LCD is 90, so you get $\frac{^-40}{90} + \frac{^-63}{90} = \frac{^-103}{90}$.

19. $(5.6) \times (^-0.11) =$

(Average Rigor) (Skill 6.3)

A. $^-0.616$

B. 0.616

C. $^-6.110$

D. 6.110

Answer A: -0.616

Simple multiplication. The answer will be negative because a positive times a negative is a negative number. $5.6 \times^- 0.11 =^- 0.616$.

20. $4\frac{2}{9} \times \frac{7}{10}$

(Rigorous) (Skill 6.3)

A. $4\frac{9}{10}$

B. $\frac{266}{90}$

C. $2\frac{43}{45}$

D. $2\frac{6}{20}$

Answer C: $2\frac{43}{45}$

Convert the mixed number to an improper fraction: $\frac{38}{9} x \frac{7}{10}$. Divide the numerator and denominator by 2 to get 19/9 x 7/5 = 133/45. Convert to a mixed number and reduce $2\frac{86}{90} = 2\frac{43}{45}$.

21. **0.74 =**
    (Easy) (Skill 6.3)

    A. $\dfrac{74}{100}$

    B. 7.4%

    C. $\dfrac{33}{50}$

    D. $\dfrac{74}{10}$

Answer A: $\dfrac{74}{100}$

This is basic conversion of decimals to fractions. 0.74→the 4 is in the hundredths place, so the answer is $\dfrac{74}{100}$.

22. $\dfrac{7}{9}+\dfrac{1}{3}\div\dfrac{2}{3}=$
    (Average Rigor) (Skill 6.3)

    A. $\dfrac{5}{3}$

    B. $\dfrac{3}{2}$

    C. 2

    D. $\dfrac{23}{18}$

Answer D: $\dfrac{23}{18}$

First, do the division.
$$\frac{1}{3}\div\frac{2}{3}=\frac{1}{3}\times\frac{3}{2}=\frac{1}{2}$$

Next, add the fractions.
$$\frac{7}{9}+\frac{1}{2}=\frac{14}{18}+\frac{9}{18}=\frac{23}{18}, \text{ which is answer D.}$$

23. **A sofa sells for $520. If the retailer makes a 30% profit, what was the wholesale price?**
    (Average Rigor) (Skill 6.3)

    A. $400

    B. $676

    C. $490

    D. $364

Answer A: $400

Let x be the wholesale price, then 1x + .30x = 520, 1.30x = 520. Divide both sides by 1.30, and x = 400 (A).

24. $(^-2.1 \times 10^4)(4.2 \times 10^{-5}) =$
    (Rigorous) (Skill 6.3)

    A.   8.82

    B.   -8.82

    C.   -0.882

    D.   0.882

Answer C: -0.882

First, multiply -2.1 x 4.2 = -8.82. Then, multiply 10^4 by 10^{-5} to get 10^{-1}. $^-8.82 \times 10^{-1} = ^- 0.882$.

25. **303 is what percent of 600?**
    (Easy) (Skill 6.3)

    A. 0.505%

    B. 5.05%

    C. 505%

    D. 50.5%

Answer D: 50.5%

Use x for the percent. $600x = 303$. $\dfrac{600x}{600} = \dfrac{303}{600} \rightarrow x = 0.505 = 50.5\%$.

26. **An item that sells for $375 is put on sale at $120. What is the percent of decrease?**
    (Average Rigor) (Skill 6.4)

    A. 25%

    B. 28%

    C. 68%

    D. 34%

Answer C: 68%

Use $(1 - x)$ as the discount. $375x = 120$.
$375(1 - x) = 120 \rightarrow 375 - 375x = 120 \rightarrow 375x = 255 \rightarrow x = 0.68 = 68\%$.

27. A restaurant employs 465 people. There are 280 waiters and 185 cooks. If 168 waiters and 85 cooks receive pay raises, what percent of the waiters received a pay raise?
(*Average Rigor*) (*Skill 6.4*)

   A. 36.13%

   B. 60%

   C. 60.22%

   D. 40%

Answer B: 60%

The total number of waiters is 280 and 168 of them get a pay raise. Divide the number getting a raise by the total number of waiters to get the percent.
$\dfrac{168}{280} = 0.6 = 60\%$.

28. The price of gas is $3.27 per gallon. Your tank holds 15 gallons of fuel. You are using two tanks a week. Approximately how much will you save weekly if the price of gas goes down to $2.30 per gallon?
(*Average Rigor*) (*Skill 6.4*)

   A. $26.00

   B. $29.00

   C. $15.00

   D. $17.00

Answer B: $29.00

15 gallons x 2 tanks = 30 gallons a week
= 30 gallons x $3.27 = $98.10
30 gallons x $2.30 = $69.00
$98.10 - $69.00 = $29.10 is approximately $29.00.

29. A boat travels 30 miles upstream in three hours. It makes the return trip in one and a half hours. What is the speed of the boat in still water?
(Average Rigor) (Skill 6.4)

   A. 10 mph

   B. 15 mph

   C. 20 mph

   D. 30 mph

Answer B: 15 mph

Let x = the speed of the boat in still water and c = the speed of the current.

	rate	time	distance
upstream	x - c	3	30
downstream	x + c	1.5	30

Solve the system:
$$3x - 3c = 30$$
$$1.5x + 1.5c = 30$$

30. Given the formula d = rt, (where d = distance, r = rate, and t = time), calculate the time required for a vehicle to travel 585 miles at a rate of 65 miles per hour.
(Average Rigor) (Skill 6.4)

   A. 8.5 hours

   B. 6.5 hours

   C. 9.5 hours

   D. 9 hours

Answer D: 9 hours

We are given d = 585 miles and r = 65 miles per hour and d = rt. Solve for t.
$$585 = 65t \rightarrow t = 9 \text{ hours.}$$

31. **Which of the equations below has $x = \dfrac{1}{6}$ as a solution?**

    i. $6x \le 4x^2 + 2$
    ii. $10x + 1 = 3(4x - 3)$
    iii. $|x - 1| = x$

    (Rigorous) (Skill 6.5)

    A. i, ii, and iii

    B. i and iii

    C. i only

    D. iii only

Answer C: i only

Substitute $x = \dfrac{1}{6}$ into each equation and solve.

i. $6\left(\dfrac{1}{6}\right) \le 4\left(\dfrac{1}{6}\right)^2 + 2 = 1 \le 4\left(\dfrac{1}{36}\right) + 2 \to 1 \le \dfrac{1}{9} + 2 \to 1 \le 2\dfrac{1}{9}$ True.

ii. $10\left(\dfrac{1}{6}\right) + 1 = 3\left(4\left(\dfrac{1}{6}\right) - 3\right) = 2\dfrac{2}{3} = 3\left(\dfrac{2}{3} - 3\right) \to 2\dfrac{2}{3} = \dfrac{6}{3} - 9 \to 2\dfrac{2}{3} = {}^{-}7$ False.

iii. $\left|\dfrac{1}{6} - 1\right| = \dfrac{1}{6} \to \left|\dfrac{1}{6} - \dfrac{6}{6}\right| = \dfrac{1}{6} \to \left|\dfrac{{}^{-}5}{6}\right| = \dfrac{1}{6} \to \dfrac{5}{6} = \dfrac{1}{6}$ False.

    So, only (i) is true, which is answer **C.**

32.   The figure below shows a running track and the shape of an inscribed rectangle with semicircles at each end.

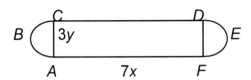

Calculate the distance around the track.
(Rigorous) (Skill 4.2)

A. $6\pi y + 14x$

B. $3\pi y + 7x$

C. $6\pi y + 7x$

D. $3\pi y + 14x$

Answer D: $3\pi y + 14x$

The two semicircles of the track create one circle with a diameter 3y. The circumference of a circle is $C = \pi d$ so $C = 3\pi y$. The length of each side of the track is 7x so the total circumference around the track is
$3\pi y + 7x + 7x = 3\pi y + 14x$.

33. **Choose the expression that is *not* equivalent to 5x + 3y + 15z:**
    (Average Rigor) (Skill 6.5)

    A. $5(x + 3z) + 3y$

    B. $3(x + y + 5z)$

    C. $3y + 5(x + 3z)$

    D. $5x + 3(y + 5z)$

Answer B: 3(x + y + 5z)

$$5x + 3y + 15z = (5x + 15z) + 3y = 5(x + 3z) + 3y \qquad \text{A. is true}$$
$$= 5x + (3y + 15z) = 5x + 3(y + 5z) \qquad \text{D. is true}$$
$$= 37 + (5x + 15z) = 37 + 5(x + 3z) \qquad \text{C. is true}$$

These can all be solved using the associative property and then factoring. However, in B. $3(x + y + 5z)$ by distributive property = 3x + 3y + 15z and does not equal 5x + 37 + 15z.

34. **Choose the equation that is equivalent to the following:**

    $$\frac{3x}{5} - 5 = 5x$$

    (Rigorous) (Skill 6.5)

    A. $3x - 25 = 25x$

    B. $x - \dfrac{25}{3} = 25x$

    C. $6x - 50 = 75x$

    D. $x + 25 = 25x$

Answer A: 3x − 25 = 25x

A is the correct answer because it is the original equation multiplied by 5. The other choices alter the answer to the original equation.

35.   If $4x - (3 - x) = 7(x - 3) + 10$, then
       (Rigorous) (Skill 6.5)

       A. $x = 8$

       B. $x = -8$

       C. $x = 4$

       D. $x = -4$

Answer C: x = 4

Solve for x.

$$4x - (3 - x) = 7(x - 3) + 10$$
$$4x - 3 + x = 7x - 21 + 10$$
$$5x - 3 = 7x - 11$$
$$5x = 7x - 11 + 3$$
$$5x - 7x = {}^{-}8$$
$${}^{-}2x = {}^{-}8$$
$$x = 4$$

36. Solve for x.

$$3x - \frac{2}{3} = \frac{5x}{2} + 2$$

(Rigorous) (Skill 6.5)

    A. $5\frac{1}{3}$

    B. $\frac{17}{3}$

    C. 2

    D. $\frac{16}{2}$

Answer A: $5\frac{1}{3}$

$$3x(6) - \frac{2}{3}(6) = \frac{5x}{2}(6) + 2(6)$$ 6 is the LCD of 2 and 3

$$18x - 4 = 15x + 12$$

$$18x = 15x + 16$$

$$3x = 16$$

$$x = \frac{16}{3} = 5\frac{1}{3}$$

37. **A family spends $150 a week for groceries. How much money is left at the end of the month?**
(Easy) (Skill 6.6)

    A. $600

    B. $150

    C. $12

    D. Not enough information

Answer D: Note enough information

The problem does not state the amount of money had at the beginning of the month.

38. **Sara travels 39 miles to class, 25 miles to work, and 14 miles to see her friend. How much does she spend in gas? Explain the operation needed for this problem.**
(Easy) (Skill 6.6)

   A. Add 39 + 25 + 14

   B. Multiply the numbers by 3

   C. Not enough information is given

   D. Add the numbers, then multiply by 5

Answer C: Not enough information is given

The problem does not state how much gas costs or how many miles Sara gets to the gallon.

39. **The teacher is introducing the concept of multiplication to her third grade students. What is another way she might write 4 x 5?**
(Easy) (Skill 6.7)

   A. 4 + 5

   B. 5 + 4

   C. 4 + 4 + 4 + 4 + 4

   D. 5 + 5 + 5 + 5 + 5

Answer C: 4 + 4 + 4 + 4 + 4

The multiplication concept can translate to an addition problem. 4 x 5 is the same as the number 4 added 5 times.

40. What is the equation that expresses the relationship between x and y in the table below?

x	y
-2	4
-1	1
0	-2
1	-5
2	-8

(Rigorous) (Skill 7.1)

A. $y = -x - 2$

B. $y = -3x - 2$

C. $y = 3x - 2$

D. $y = \dfrac{1}{3}x - 1$

Answer B: $y = -3x - 2$

Solve by plugging in the values of x and y into the equations to see if they work. The answer is B because it is the only equation for which the values of x and y are correct.

41. Given $f(x) = (x)^3 - 3(x)^2 + 5$, find $x = (-2)$.
    (Rigorous) (Skill 7.1)

    A. 15

    B. -15

    C. 25

    D. -25

Answer B: -15

Substitute $x = -2$.
$$f(-2) = (^-2)^3 - 3 \times (^-2)^2 + 5$$
$$f(-2) = ^- 8 - 3(4) + 5$$
$$f(-2) = ^- 8 - 12 + 5$$
$$f(-2) = ^- 15$$

42. $(^-2.1 \times 10^4)(4.2 \times 10^{-5}) =$
    (Rigorous) (Skill 7.2)

    A. 8.82

    B. -8.82

    C. -0.882

    D. 0.882

Answer C: -0.882

First, multiply -2.1 and 4.2 to get -8.82. Then, multiply 10^4 by 10^{-5} to get 10^{-1}. $^-8.82 \times 10^{-1} = ^- 0.882$.

43. $-9\frac{1}{4}$ ☐ $-8\frac{2}{3}$

(Average Rigor) (Skill 7.3)

A. =

B. <

C. >

D. ≤

Answer B: <

The larger the absolute value of a negative number, the smaller the negative number is. The absolute value of $-9\frac{1}{4}$ is $9\frac{1}{4}$ which is larger than the absolute value of $-8\frac{2}{3}$ is $8\frac{2}{3}$. Therefore, the sign should be $-9\frac{1}{4} < -8\frac{2}{3}$.

44.   **Choose the expression that is *not* equivalent to 5x + 3y + 15z:**
(Average Rigor) (Skill 7.4)

A. 5(x + 3z) + 3y

B. 3(x + y + 5z)

C. 3y + 5(x + 3z)

D. 5x + 3(y + 5z)

Answer B: 3(x + y + 5z)

5x + 3y + 15z = (5x + 15z) + 3y = 5(x + 3z) + 3y   A. is true
= 5x + (3y + 15z) = 5x + 3(y + 5z)   D. is true
= 37 + (5x + 15z) = 37 + 5(x + 3z)   C. is true

These can all be solved using the associative property and then factoring. However, in B. 3(x + y + 5z) by distributive property = 3x + 3y + 15z does not equal 5x + 37 + 15z.

45. Round $1\frac{13}{16}$ of an inch to the nearest quarter of an inch.

   (Easy) (Skill 7.5)

   A. $1\frac{1}{4}$ inch

   B. $1\frac{5}{8}$ inch

   C. $1\frac{3}{4}$ inch

   D. 2 inches

Answer C: $1\frac{3}{4}$ inch

$1\frac{13}{16}$ inches is approximately $1\frac{12}{16}$, which is also $1\frac{3}{4}$, which is the nearest $\frac{1}{4}$ of an inch, so the answer is C.

46.   Set A, B, C, and U are related as shown in the diagram.

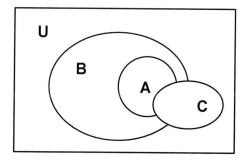

Which of the following is true, assuming not one of the six regions is empty?
(Average Rigor) (Skill 7.6)

A. Any element that is a member of set B is also a member of set A.

B. No element is a member of all three sets A, B, and C.

C. Any element that is a member of set U is also a member of set B.

D. None of the above statements is true.

Answer D: None of the above statements is true.

A, B and C are not true. Therefore, D is the answer.

47. **Select the statement that is the negation of the statement, "If the weather is cold, then the soccer game will be played."**
(Average Rigor) (Skill 7.6)

   A. If the weather is not cold, then the soccer game will be played.

   B. The weather is cold and the soccer game will not be played.

   C. If the soccer game is played, then the weather is not cold.

   D. The weather is cold and the soccer game will be played.

Answer B: The weather is cold and the soccer game will not be played.

Negation of "if p, then q" is "p and (not q)."

48. **Study the information given below. If a logical conclusion is given, select that conclusion.**

   Bob eats donuts or he eats yogurt. If Bob eats yogurt, then he is healthy. If Bob is healthy, then he can run the marathon. Bob does not eat yogurt.
   (Average Rigor) (Skill 7.6)

   A. Bob does not eat donuts.

   B. Bob is healthy.

   C. Bob runs the marathon.

   D. None of the above.

Answer D: None of the above.

Use Disjunctive Syllogism: p or q
                             not p
                             therefore, q

The fact that Bob does not eat yogurt means that he eats donuts. Because he eats donuts, Option A is incorrect. In addition, Bob is not healthy (B) or running a marathon (C), because he would have to eat yogurt for these things to happen. So the answer is D.

49. **Select the statement below that is NOT logically equivalent to "If Mary works late, then Bill will prepare lunch."**
   (Average Rigor) (Skill 7.6)

   A. Bill prepares lunch or Mary does not work late.

   B. If Bill does not prepare lunch, then Mary did not work late.

   C. If Bill prepares lunch, then Mary works late.

   D. Mary does not work late or Bill prepares lunch.

Answer C: If Bill prepares lunch, then Mary works late.

The second statement must also be an "if, then" statement to be logically equivalent to the first. Use the Law of Contraposition: If p, then q – not q, so, therefore, not p.

50. **Select the rule of logical equivalence that directly (in one step) transforms the statement (i) into statement (ii),**

   i. **Not all the students have books.**
   ii. **Some students do not have books.**
   (Average Rigor) (Skill 7.6)

   A. "If p, then q" is equivalent to "if not q, then b."

   B. "Not all are p" is equivalent to "some are not p."

   C. "Not q" is equivalent to "p."

   D. "All are not p" is equivalent to "none are p."

Answer B: "Not all are p" is equivalent to "some are not p."

Identify the quantifiers, *all* and *some*. The negation of "not all have" is "some do not have." *Not all* students *have* books; therefore, *some* students *do not* have books.

51. **Given that:**
    i. No athletes are weak.
    ii. All football players are athletes.

    Determine which conclusion can be logically deduced.
    (Average Rigor) (Skill 7.6)

    A. Some football players are weak.

    B. All football players are weak.

    C. No football player is weak.

    D. None of the above is true.

Answer C: No football player is weak.

Use the Law of Syllogism: If p, then q
                          If q, then r
                          Therefore if p, then r

In "if, then" form this would be, "If you are an athlete, then you are not weak. If you are a football player, then you are an athlete." Clearly, if you are a football player, you are an athlete, which means you are also not weak.

52. **What is missing from the following graph?**

Cars Sold

```
              |  X
   X          |  X
   X          |  X
   X    X     |  X
   X    X     |  X
   X    X     |  X
   X    X   X |  X
  2005 2006 2007 2008
```

(Easy) (Skill 7.7)

A. Total number of cars sold

B. Kinds of cars

C. The value of X (interval)

D. Time period covered

Answer C: The value of X (interval)

This graph does not give a value on the left for each X or the interval used. A proportion can be calculated but not an actual value.

53. The following chart shows the yearly average number of international tourists visiting Redondo Beach for 1990-1994. How many more international tourists visited Redondo Beach in 1994 than in 1991?
(Easy) (Skill 7.8)

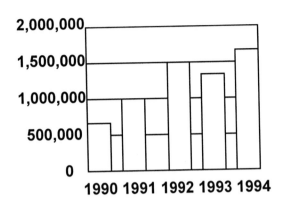

A. 100,000

B. 600,000

C. 1,600,000

D. 8,000,000

Answer B: 600,000

The number of tourists in 1991 was 1,000,000 and the number in 1994 was 1,600,000. Subtract to get a difference of 600,000.

54. **Consider the graph of the distribution of the length of time it took individuals to complete an employment form.**

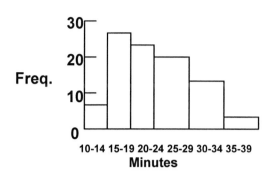

Approximately how many individuals took less than 15 minutes to complete the employment form?
(Easy) (Skill 7.8)

A. 35

B. 28

C. 7

D. 4

Answer C: 7

According to the chart, the number of people who took less than 15 minutes is less than 10 and more than 5. So (C) 7 is the best estimate.

55. **Which statement is true about George's budget?**
   (Easy) (Skill 7.8)

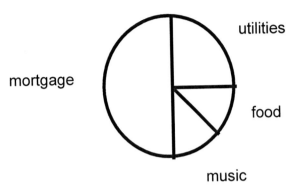

A. George spends the greatest portion of his income on food.

B. George spends twice as much on utilities as he does on his mortgage.

C. George spends twice as much on utilities as he does on food.

D. George spends the same amount on food and utilities as he does on his mortgage.

Answer C: George spends twice as much on utilities as he does on food.

George spends the most on his mortgage, and he spends half as much on utilities as on his mortgage. Food and utilities make up one-third of his spending, while the mortgage is half. George spends twice as much on utilities as he does on food.

56. The table below shows the distribution of majors for a group of college students.

Major	Proportion of students
Mathematics	0.32
Photography	0.26
Journalism	0.19
Engineering	0.21
Criminal Law	0.02

If it is known that a student chosen at random is not majoring in mathematics or engineering, what is the probability that a student is majoring in journalism?
(Rigorous) (Skill 7.8)

A. 0.19

B. 0.36

C. 0.40

D. 0.81

Answer C: 0.40

The proportion of students majoring in math or engineering is $0.32 + 0.21 = 0.53$. This means that the proportion of students NOT majoring in math or engineering is $1.00 - 0.53 = 0.47$. The proportion of students majoring in journalism out of those not majoring in math or engineering is $\dfrac{0.19}{0.47} = 0.404$.

COMPETENCY 8.0   WRITING THE ESSAY

The Writing Test is a one-hour test consisting of two essay questions. One of the essay questions asks examinees to write about a remembered experience. The other question is designed to elicit expository prose that will permit writers to demonstrate their analytical skills.

ABILITIES SPECIFICATIONS

The questions in the Writing Test will elicit a writing sample that will demonstrate the following traits:

1. clarity (i.e., readers can comprehend immediately what is meant),
2. focus (i.e., readers are kept on track),
3. development through appropriate support or illustration,
4. reasonable mastery of the conventions of standard written English,
5 prose essentially free from non sequiturs, internal contradictions, unwarranted conclusions, and confusion of fact and opinion.

TOPIC SPECIFICATIONS
Topics should be of the following two types:

TYPE I (one question per examination):
Topics should elicit a sample of expressive writing about a remembered experience (expressive aim).

TYPE II (one question per examination):
Topics should elicit a sample of expository writing that will permit the examinees to demonstrate their analytic skills (referential aim).

GENERAL STRATEGIES FOR WRITING THE ESSAY

1. Watch the time.	Use *all* the time wisely. You shouldn't run out of time, nor should you write an incomplete essay because you didn't use all the time allowed.
2. Read the instructions carefully, and select one of the topics.	Determine what the topic is asking. Think of how the topic relates to what you know, to what you have learned, and to what related prior experiences you have had so that you can provide concrete details rather than vague generalities.
3. Take a few minutes to prewrite.	Jot down your first ideas. Sketch a quick outline, or group your ideas together with arrows or numbers.
4. Write a thesis statement that provides a clear focus for your essay.	State a point of view in your thesis that guides the purpose and scope of your essay. Consider the larger point you're trying to convey to readers and what you want readers to understand about the topic. Avoid a thesis statement framed as a fact, a question, or an announcement.
5. Develop the essay considering your purpose.	Develop paragraphs fully; give examples and reasons that support your thesis. Indent each new paragraph. Note that a good essay may be longer or shorter than the basic five-paragraph format of some short essays. The key is to **develop** a topic by using concrete, informative details.
6. Tie your main ideas together with a brief conclusion.	Provide a concluding paragraph that ties together the essay's points and offers insights about the topic. Avoid a conclusion that merely restates the thesis and repeats the supporting details.
7. Revise and proofread the essay so that it conforms to standard American English.	Look for particular errors you tend to make. Mark errors and correct them. You'll never be penalized for clearly crossing out errors. Look for words, sentences, or even paragraphs that need changing. Write legibly so that readers can easily decipher what you have written.

Topic Analysis

Even before you select a topic, determine what each prompt is asking you to discuss. This first decision is crucial. If you pick a topic that you don't really understand or about which you have little to say, you'll have difficulty developing your essay. So take a few moments to analyze each topic carefully *before* you begin to write.

Topic A: a modern invention that can be considered a wonder of the world

In general, the topic prompts have two parts:
        the *SUBJECT* of the topic and
        an *ASSERTION* about the subject.

The **subject** is *a modern invention*. In this prompt, the word *modern* indicates that you should discuss something invented recently, at least in this century. The word *invention* indicates that you're to write about something created by humans (not some natural phenomena such as mountains or volcanoes). You may discuss an invention that has potential for harm, such as chemical weaponry or the atomic bomb; or you may discuss an invention that has the potential for good: the computer, DNA testing, television, antibiotics, and so on.

The **assertion** (a statement of point of view) is that *the invention has such powerful or amazing qualities that it should be considered a wonder of the world*. The assertion states your point of view about the subject, and it limits the range for discussion. In other words, you would discuss particular qualities or uses of the invention, not how it was invented or whether it should have been invented at all.

Note also that this particular topic encourages you to use examples to show readers that a particular invention is a modern wonder. Some topic prompts lend themselves to essays with an argumentative edge, one in which you take a stand on a particular issue and persuasively prove your point. Here, you undoubtedly should offer examples and illustrations of the many wonders and uses of the particular invention you chose.

Be aware that misreading or misinterpreting the topic prompt can lead to serious problems. Papers that do not address the topic can occur from reading too quickly, jumping to conclusions, and only half-understanding the topic. This type of misreading can also lead to a paper that addresses only part of the topic prompt rather than the entire topic.

Formulate a thesis or statement of main idea

To develop a complete essay, spend a few minutes planning. Jot down your ideas, and quickly sketch an outline. Although you may feel under pressure to begin writing, you will write more effectively if you plan your major points.

Prewriting
Before actually writing, you'll need to generate content and to develop a writing plan. Three prewriting techniques that can be helpful follow:

Brainstorming

When brainstorming, quickly create a list of words and ideas that are connected to the topic. Let your mind roam freely to generate as many relevant ideas as possible in a few minutes. For example, on the topic of computers you may write

    computer- modern invention
    types- personal computers, micro-chips in calculators and watches
    wonder - acts like an electronic brain
    uses - science, medicine, offices, homes, schools
    problems- too much reliance; the machines aren't perfect

This list could help you focus on the topic and states the points you could develop in the body paragraphs. The brainstorming list keeps you on track and is well worth the few minutes it takes to jot down the ideas. While you haven't ordered the ideas, seeing them on paper is an important step.

Questioning

Questioning helps you focus as you mentally ask a series of exploratory questions about the topic. You may use the most basic questions: **who, what, where, when, why, and how.**

"**What** is my subject?"
    [computers]

"**What** types of computers are there?"
    [personal computers, micro-chip computers]

"**How** have computers been a positive invention?"
    [act like an electronic brain in machinery and equipment; help solve complex scientific problems]

"How have computers been a positive invention?"
[used to make improvements in:

- science (space exploration, moon landings)
- medicine (MRIs, CAT scans, surgical tools, research models)
- business (PCs, FAX, telephone equipment)
- education (computer programs for math, languages, science, social studies), and
- personal use (family budgets, tax programs, healthy diet plans)]

"How can I show that computers are good?"
[citing numerous examples]

"What problems do I see with computers?"
[too much reliance; not yet perfect]

"What personal experiences would help me develop examples to respond to this topic?
[my own experiences using computers]

Of course, you may not have time to write out the questions completely. You might just write the words *who, what, where, why, how* and the major points next to each. An abbreviated list might look as follows:

What — computers/modern wonder/making life better
How — through technological improvements: lasers, calculators, CAT scans, MRIs.

Where – in science and space exploration, medicine, schools, offices

In a few moments, your questions should help you to focus on the topic and to generate interesting ideas and points to make in the essay. Later in the writing process, you can look back at the list to be sure you've made the key points that you had intended to make.

Clustering

Some visual thinkers find clustering an effective prewriting method. When clustering, you draw a box in the center of your paper and write your topic within that box. Then you draw lines from the center box and connect it to small satellite boxes that contain related ideas. See the cluster example that follows on computers:

SAMPLE CLUSTER

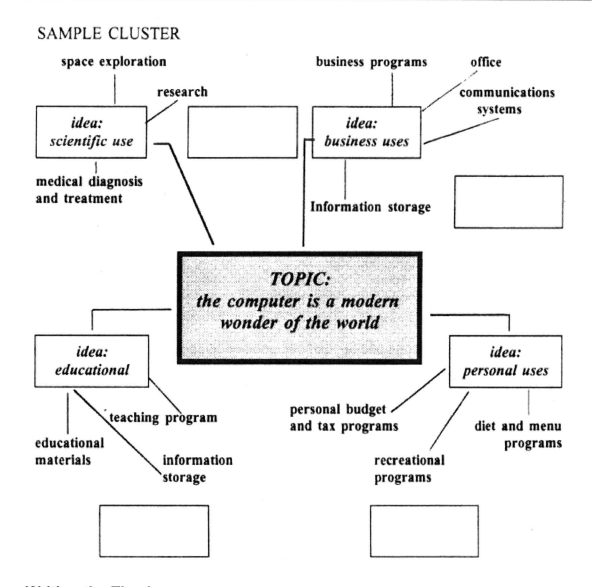

space exploration

research

idea:
scientific use

medical diagnosis
and treatment

business programs

office

communications
systems

idea:
business uses

Information storage

TOPIC:
the computer is a modern
wonder of the world

idea:
educational

teaching program

educational
materials

information
storage

personal budget
and tax programs

recreational
programs

idea:
personal uses

diet and menu
programs

Writing the Thesis

After focusing on the topic and generating your ideas, form your thesis, the controlling idea of your essay. The thesis is your general statement to the reader expressing your point of view and guiding your essay's purpose and scope. The thesis should allow you either to explain your subject or to take an arguable position about it. A strong thesis statement is neither too narrow nor too broad.

Subject and Assertion of the Thesis

From the analysis of the general topic, you saw the topic in terms of its two parts - *subject* and *assertion*. On the exam, your thesis or viewpoint on a particular topic is stated in two important points:

1. the *SUBJECT* of the paper
2. the *ASSERTION* about the subject.

The **subject of the thesis** relates directly to the topic prompt, but expresses the specific area you have chosen to discuss. (Remember that the exam topic will be general and will allow you to choose a particular subject related to the topic). For example, the computer is one modern invention.

The **assertion of the thesis** is your viewpoint, or opinion, about the subject. The assertion provides the motive or purpose for your essay, and it may be an arguable point or one that explains or illustrates a point of view.

For example, you may present an argument for or against a particular issue. You may contrast two people, objects, or methods to show that one is better than the other. You may analyze a situation in all aspects and make recommendations for improvement. You may assert that a law or policy should be adopted, changed, or abandoned. You may also, as in the computer example, explain to your reader that a situation or condition exists; rather than argue a viewpoint, you would use examples to illustrate your assertion about the essay's subject.

Specifically, the **subject** of Topic A is *the computer*. The **assertions** are that *it is a modern wonder that has improved our lives* **and** *that we have come to rely on*. Now you quickly have created a workable thesis in a few moments:

> *The computer is a modern wonder of the world that has improved our lives and that we have come to rely on.*

Guidelines for Writing Thesis Statements

The following guidelines are not a formula for writing thesis statements, but they are general strategies for making your thesis statement clearer and more effective.

1. State a *particular point* of *view* about the topic with both a *subject* and an *assertion.* The thesis should give the essay purpose and scope and thus provide readers a guide. If the thesis is vague, your essay may be undeveloped because you do not have an idea to assert or a point to explain. Weak thesis statements are often framed as facts, questions, or announcements:

    a. Avoid a statement of fact as a thesis. While a statement of fact may provide a subject, it generally does not include a point of view about the subject that provides the basis for an extended discussion. Example: *Recycling saved our community over $10,000 last year.* This fact provides a detail, *not* a point of view. Such a detail might be found within an essay, but it does not state a point of view.

    b. Avoid framing the thesis as a vague question. In many cases, rhetorical questions do not provide a clear point of view for an extended essay. Example: *How do people recycle?* This question neither asserts a point of view nor helpfully guides the reader to understand the essay's purpose and scope.

    c. Avoid the "announcer" topic sentence that merely states the topic you will discuss
    Example: I *will discuss ways to recycle.* This sentence states the subject, but the scope of the essay is only suggested. Again, this statement does not assert a viewpoint that guides the essay's purpose. It merely "announces" that the writer will write about the topic.

2. Start with a workable thesis. You might revise your thesis after you begin writing because you discover a more interesting point of view.

3. If feasible and appropriate, perhaps state the thesis in multi-point form, expressing the scope of the essay. By stating the points in parallel form, you clearly lay out the essay's plan for the reader.
    Example: *To improve the environment, we can recycle our trash, elect politicians who see the environment as a priority, and support lobbying groups who work for environmental protection.*

4. Because of the exam time limit, place your thesis in the first paragraph to alert readers to the essay's main idea.

Organize ideas and details effectively

Creating a working outline

A good thesis gives structure to your essay and helps focus your thoughts. When forming your thesis, look at your prewriting strategy – clustering, questioning, or brainstorming. Then decide quickly which two or three major areas you'll discuss. Remember that you must limit *the scope* of the paper because of the time factor.

The **outline** lists those main areas or points as topics for each paragraph. Looking at the prewriting cluster on computers, you might choose several areas in which computers help us, for examples, in science and medicine, business, and education. You might also consider people's reliance on this "wonder" and include at least one paragraph about this reliance. A formal outline for this essay might look like the one below:

I.   Introduction and thesis
II. Computers used in science and medicine
II. Computers used in business
IV. Computers used in education
V. People's reliance on computers
VI. Conclusion

Under time pressure, however, you may use a shorter organizational plan, such as abbreviated key words in a list. For example

1. intro: wonders of the computer OR
2. science
3. med
4. schools
5. business
6. conclusion

a. intro: wonders of computers - science
b. in the space industry
c. in medical technology
d. conclusion

Developing the essay

With a working thesis and outline, you can begin writing the essay. The essay should be in three main sections:

1) The **introduction** sets up the essay and leads to the thesis statement.
2) The **body paragraphs** are developed with concrete information supporting the **topic sentences**.
3) The **conclusion** ties the essay together.

Introduction

Put your thesis statement into a clear, coherent opening paragraph. One effective device is to use a funnel approach in which you begin with a brief description of the broader issue and then move to a clearly focused, specific thesis statement.

Consider the following introductions for the essay on computers. The length of each is an obvious difference. Read each, and consider the other differences.

> Does each introduce the subject generally?
> Does each lead to a stated thesis?
> Does each relate to the topic prompt?

Introduction 1: *Computers are used every day. They have many uses. Some people who use them are workers, teachers, and doctors.*

Analysis: This introduction does give the general topic, computers used every day, but it does not explain what those uses are. This introduction does not offer a point of view in a clearly stated thesis, nor does it convey the idea that computers are a modem wonder.

Introduction 2: *Computers are used just about everywhere these days. I don't think there's an office around that doesn't use computers, and we use them a lot in all kinds of jobs. Computers are great for making life easier and work better. I don't think we'd get along without the computer.*

Analysis: This introduction gives the general topic about computers and mentions one area that uses computers. The thesis states that people couldn't get along without computers, but it does not state the specific areas the essay discusses. Note, too, the meaning is not helped by vague diction such as *a lot* or *great.*

Introduction 3: *Each day, we either use computers or see them being used around us. We wake to the sound of a digital alarm operated by a micro-chip. Our cars run by computerized machinery. We use computers to help us learn. We receive phone calls and letters transferred from computers across continents. Our astronauts walked on the moon and returned safely because of computer technology. The computer is a wonderful electronic brain that we have come to rely on, and it has changed our world through advances in science, business, and education.*

Analysis: This introduction is the most thorough and fluent because it generates interest in the general topic and offers specific information about computers as a modern wonder. It also leads to a thesis that directs the reader to the scope of the discussion--advances in science, business, and education.

Topic Sentences

Just as the essay must have an overall focus reflected in the thesis statement, each paragraph must have a central idea reflected in the topic sentence. A good topic sentence also provides transitions that establish links with previous paragraphs and relate to the essay's thesis. Good topic sentences, therefore, provide unity throughout the essay.

Consider the following potential topic sentences. Be sure that each provides transitions and clearly states the subject of the paragraph.

Topic Sentence 1: *Computers are used in science.*

Analysis: This sentence simply states the topic--computers used in science. It does not relate to the thesis or provide links with the introduction. The reader still does not know how computers are used.

Topic Sentence 2: *Now I will talk about computers used in science.*

Analysis: Like the faulty "announcer" thesis statement, this "announcer" topic sentence is vague and merely names the topic.

Topic Sentence 3: *First, computers used in science have improved our lives.*

Analysis: The transition word *First* helps link the introduction and this paragraph. It adds unity to the essay. It does not, however, give specifics about the improvements that computers have made in our lives.

Topic Sentence 4: *First used in scientific research and spaceflights, computers are now used extensively in the diagnosis and treatment of disease.*

Analysis: This sentence is the most thorough and fluent. It provides specific areas that will be discussed in the paragraph and offers more than an announcement of the topic. The writer gives concrete information about the content of the paragraph that will follow.

Summary Guidelines for Writing Topic Sentences
1. Specifically relate the topic to the thesis statement.
2. State clearly and concretely the subject of the paragraph.
3. Incorporate some transitional strategies.
4. Avoid topic sentences that are facts, questions, or announcers.

3. Develop the ideas in the writing through support or illustration.

Supporting Details

If you have a good thesis and a good outline, you should be able to construct a complete essay. Your paragraphs should contain concrete, interesting information and supporting details to support your point of view. As often as possible, create images in your readers' minds. Fact statements add weight to your opinions, especially when you are trying to convince readers of your viewpoint. Because every good thesis has an assertion, you should offer specifics, facts, data, anecdotes, expert opinion, and other details to *show* or *prove* that assertion. While *you* know what you mean, your *readers* do not. On the exam, you must explain and develop ideas as fully as possible in the time allowed.

In the following paragraph, the sentences in **bold print** provide a skeleton of a paragraph on the benefits of recycling. The sentences in bold are generalizations that by themselves do not explain the need to recycle. The sentences in *italics* add details to show the general points in bold. Notice how the supporting details help you understand the necessity for recycling.

While one day recycling may become mandatory in all states, right now it is voluntary in many communities. *Those of us who participate in recycling are amazed by how much material is recycled.* **For many communities, the blue-box recycling program has had an immediate effect.** *By just recycling glass, aluminum cans, and plastic bottles, we have reduced the volume of disposable trash by one third, thus extending the useful life of local landfills by over a decade. Imagine the difference if those dramatic results were achieved nationwide.* **The amount of reusable items we thoughtlessly dispose of is staggering.** *For example, Americans dispose of enough steel every day to supply Detroit car manufacturers for three months. Additionally, we dispose of enough aluminum annually to rebuild the nation's air fleet. These statistics, available from the Environmental Protection Agency (EPA), should encourage all of us to watch what we throw away.* **Clearly, recycling in our homes and in our communities directly improves the environment.**

Notice how the author's supporting examples enhance the message of the paragraph and relate to the author's thesis noted above. If you only read the bold-face sentences, you have a glimpse at the topic. This paragraph of illustration, however, is developed through numerous details creating specific images: *reduced the volume of disposable trash by one-third; extended the useful life of local landfills by over a decade; enough steel every day to supply Detroit car manufacturers for three months; enough aluminum to rebuild the nation's air fleet.* If the writer had merely written a few general sentences, then you would not fully understand the vast amount of trash involved in recycling or the positive results of current recycling efforts.

End your essay with a brief, straightforward **concluding paragraph** that ties together the essay's content and leaves the reader with a sense of completion. The conclusion should reinforce the main points, offer some insight into the topic, provide a sense of unity for the essay by relating it to the thesis, and signal closure.

Consistent Point of View

Point of view defines the focus a writer assumes in relation to a given topic. It is extremely important to maintain a consistent point of view in order to create coherent paragraphs. Point of view is related to matters of person, tense, tone, and number.

Person – A shift in the form which indicates whether a person is speaking (first), is being spoken to (second), or is being spoken about (third) can disrupt continuity of a passage. In your essay, it is recommended that you write in the third person because it is often considered to be the most formal of the modes of person. If you do decide to use the more informal first or second person (I, you, we) in your essay, be careful not to shift between first, second, and third persons from sentence to sentence or paragraph to paragraph.

Tense – Verbs tenses indicate the time of an action or state of being – the past, present, or future. It is important to consistently stick to a selected tense, though there may be conscious deviations to express specialized information. For instance, in an essay about the history of environmental protection, it might be strategic to include a paragraph about the future benefits of protecting Earth.

Tone – The tone of an essay varies greatly with the purpose, subject, and audience. It is best to assume a formal tone for this essay. (See Domain II, COMPETENCY 2.3).

Number – Words change when their meanings are singular or plural. Make sure that you do not shift number carelessly; if a meaning is singular in one sentence, do not make it plural in a subsequent sentence.

On the next page is a sample strong response to the prompt:
A problem people recognize and should do something about

Sample Strong Response

Does the introduction help orient the reader to the topic?

Time magazine, which typically selects a person of the year, chose Earth as the planet of the year in 1988 to underscore the severe problems facing our planet and, therefore, us. We hear dismal reports every day about the water shortage, the ozone depletion, and the obscene volume of trash generated by our society. Because the problem is global, many people feel powerless to help. Fortunately, by being environmentally aware, we can take steps to alter what seems inevitable. We can recycle our trash and support politicians and lobbying groups who will work for laws to protect the environment.

Is there a thesis? Does it clearly state the main idea of the essay?

While one day recycling may be mandatory in all states, right now it is voluntary in many communities. Those of us who participate in recycling are amazed by how much material is recycled. For many communities, the blue box recycling program has had an immediate effect. Just by recycling glass, aluminum cans, and plastic bottles, we have reduced the volume of disposable trash by one-third, thus extending the useful life of local landfills by over a decade. Imagine the difference if those dramatic results were achieved nationwide. The amount of reusable items we thoughtlessly dispose of is staggering. For example, Americans dispose of enough steel every day to supply Detroit car manufacturers for three months. Additionally, we dispose of enough aluminum annually to rebuild the nation's air fleet. These statistics, available from the Environmental Protection Agency (EPA), should encourage us to watch what we throw away. Clearly, recycling in our homes and communities directly improves the environment.

Does each paragraph have a topic sentence that provides transition and defines the idea?

Do the paragraphs purposefully support the thesis? Do they have interesting details and examples?

Are the paragraphs unified and coherent? Is the material in each paragraph relevant and important?

Moreover, we must be aware of the political issues involved in environmental protection because, unfortunately, the environmental crisis continues despite policies and laws on the books. Enacted in the 1970s, the federal Clean Water Act was intended to clean up polluted water throughout the nation and to provide safe drinking water for everyone. However, today, with the Water Act still in place, dangerous medical waste has washed onto public beaches in California; and, recently, several people died from the polluted drinking water in Madison, Wisconsin. Additionally, contradictory governmental policies often work against resource protection. For example, some state welfare agencies give new mothers money only for disposable, not cloth, diapers. In fact, consumer groups found that cloth diapers are cheaper initially and save money over time as we struggle with the crisis of bulging landfills. Clearly, we need consistent government policies and stiffer laws to ensure mandatory enforcement and heavy fines for polluters. We can do this best by electing politicians who will fight for such laws and voting out those who won't.

Does the conclusion tie the essay together?

We can also work to save our planet by supporting organizations that lobby for meaningful, enforceable legal changes. Most of us do not have time to write letters, send telegrams, or study every issue concerning the environment. We can join organizations that act as watchdogs for us all. For example, organizations such as Greenpeace, the Cousteau Society, and the Sierra Club all offer memberships for as low as $15. By supporting these organizations, we ensure that they have the necessary resources to keep working for all of us and do not have to lower their standards to remain viable.

Is the essay edited for grammar and mechanical errors?

Clearly, we all must become environmentally aware. Only through increased awareness can we avoid the tragic consequences stemming from pollution and mindless consumption of resources. We must actively support recycling programs and support those who fight to protect our fragile environment.

Analysis: While not every essay needs to be this thorough in order to pass the exam, this essay shows that with a clear thesis and concept in mind, a writer can produce a literate, interesting piece at one sitting. The introduction creates interest in the general topic and leads to a thesis in the last sentence. The reader has a very clear idea of what will be addressed in the essay, and all body paragraphs have topic sentences that relate to the thesis and provide transitional linkage. The numerous supporting details and examples are presented in a sophisticated style that reads easily and is enhanced by a college-level vocabulary and word choice. Transitional words and phrases add unity to sentences and paragraphs. Grammar and mechanics are correct, so errors don't detract from the force of the message. For all these reasons, this essay is a polished piece of writing deserving of an upper-range score.

CONVENTIONS OF STANDARD WRITTEN ENGLISH

Sentence structure

Recognize simple, compound, complex, and compound-complex sentences. Use dependent (subordinate) and independent clauses correctly to create these sentence structures.

Simple – Consists of one independent clause
>   Joyce wrote a letter.

Compound – Consists of two or more independent clauses. The two clauses are usually connected by a coordinating conjunction **preceded by a comma** (and, but, or, nor, for, so, yet). Compound sentences are sometimes connected by semicolons.
>   Joyce wrote a letter, and Dot drew a picture.

Complex- Consists of an independent clause plus one or more dependent clauses. The dependent clause may precede the independent clause or follow it.
>   While Joyce wrote a letter, Dot drew a picture.

Compound/Complex – Consists of one or more dependent clauses plus two or more independent clauses.

>   When Mother asked the girls to demonstrate their skills, Joyce wrote a letter, and Dot drew a picture.

Note: Do **not** confuse compound sentence elements with compound sentences.

>   Simple sentence with compound subject
>> Joyce and Dot wrote letters.
>> The girl in row three and the boy next to her were passing notes across the aisle.

>   Simple sentence with compound predicate
>> Joyce wrote letters and drew pictures.
>> The captain of the high school debate team graduated with honors and studied broadcast journalism in college.

>   Simple sentence with compound object of preposition
>> Colleen graded the students' essays for style and mechanical accuracy.

Types of Clauses

Clauses are connected word groups that are composed of *at least* one subject and one verb. (A subject is the doer of an action or the element that is being joined. A verb conveys either the action or the link.)

Students are waiting for the start of the assembly.
Subject   Verb

At the end of the play, students wait for the curtain to come down.
                    Subject Verb

Clauses can be independent or dependent.

Independent clauses can stand alone or can be joined to other clauses.

Independent clause	for and nor	
Independent clause,	but or yet so	Independent clause
Independent clause	;	Independent clause
Dependent clause	,	Independent clause
Independent clause		Dependent clause

Dependent clauses, by definition, contain at least one subject and one verb. However, they cannot stand alone as a complete sentence. They are dependent on the main clause.

There are two types of dependent clauses: (1) those with a subordinating conjunction, and (2) those with a relative pronoun

Sample subordinating conjunctions:

Although
When
If
Unless
Because

Unless a cure is discovered, many more people will die of the disease.
Dependent clause   +   Independent clause

Sample relative pronouns:

Who
Whom
Which
That

The White House has an official website that contains press releases, news updates, and biographies of the President and Vice-President.
(Independent clause + relative pronoun + relative dependent clause)

Recognize correct placement of modifiers

Participial phrases that are not placed near the word they modify often create confusion. They are called misplaced modifiers. Participial phrases that do not relate to the subject being modified create confusion. They are called dangling modifiers.

Error: Weighing the options carefully, a decision was made regarding the punishment of the convicted murderer.

Problem: Who is weighing the options? No one capable of weighing is named in the sentence; thus, the participial phrase *weighing the options carefully* dangles. This problem can be corrected by adding a subject of the sentence capable of doing the action.

Correction: *Weighing the options carefully, **the judge** made a decision regarding the punishment of the convicted murderer.*

Error: Returning to my favorite watering hole brought back many fond memories.

Problem: The person who returned is never indicated, and the participial phrase dangles. This problem can be corrected by creating a dependent clause from the modifying phrase.

Correction: *When I returned to my favorite watering hole, many fond memories came back to me.*

Error: One damaged house stood only to remind townspeople of the hurricane.

Problem: The misplacement of the modifier *only* suggests that the sole reason the house remained was to serve as a reminder, creating ambiguity.

Correction: *Only one damaged house stood, reminding townspeople of the hurricane.*

Error: Recovered from the five-mile hike, the obstacle course was a piece of cake for the Boy Scout troop.

Problem: The obstacle course did not recover from the five-mile hike, so the modifying phrase must be placed closer to the word *troop* for clarity.

Correction: *The obstacle course was a piece of cake for the Boy Scout troop, which had just recovered from a five-mile hike.*

Faulty parallelism

Two or more elements stated in a single clause should be expressed with the same (or parallel) structure (e.g., all adjectives, all verb forms, or all nouns).

Error: She needed to be beautiful, successful, and have fame.

Problem: The phrase to be is followed by two different structures: *beautiful* and *successful* are adjectives, and *have fame* is a verb phrase.

Correction: *She needed to be <u>beautiful</u>, <u>successful</u>, and <u>famous</u>.*
        (adjective) (adjective)   (adjective)
                      OR
She needed <u>beauty</u>, <u>success</u>, and <u>fame</u>.
      (noun)   (noun)   (noun)

Error: I plan either to sell my car during the spring or during the summer.

Problem: Paired conjunctions (also called correlative conjunctions - such as either-or, both-and, neither-nor, not only-but also) need to be followed with similar structures. In the sentence above, *either* is followed by *to sell my car during the spring*, while *or* is followed only by the phrase *during the summer*.

Correction: *I plan to sell my car during either the spring or the summer.*

Error: The President pledged to lower taxes and that he would cut spending to lower the national debt.

Problem: Since the infinitive phrase *to lower taxes* follows the verb *pledged*, an infinitive phrase *to cut spending* is needed for parallelism.

Correction: *The President pledged to lower taxes and to cut spending in order to lower the national debt.*

                              OR

The President pledged that he would lower taxes and cut spending to lower the national debt.

Fragments, comma splices, and run-on sentences

Fragments occur (1) if word groups standing alone are missing either a subject or a verb, and (2) if word groups containing a subject and verb and standing alone are actually made dependent because of the use of subordinating conjunctions or relative pronouns.

Error: The teacher waiting for the class to complete the assignment.

Problem: This sentence is not complete because an *-ing* word alone does not function as a verb. When a helping verb is added (for example, was waiting), it will become a sentence.

Correction: *The teacher was waiting for the class to complete the assignment.*

Error: Until the last toy was removed from the floor.

Problem: Words such as *until, because, although, when,* and *if* make a clause dependent and, thus, incapable of standing alone. An independent clause must be added to make the sentence complete.

Correction: *Until the last toy was removed from the floor, the kids could not go outside to play.*

Error: The city will close the public library. Because of a shortage of funds.

Problem: The problem is the same as above. The dependent clause must be joined to the independent clause.

Correction: *The city will close the public library because of a shortage of funds.*

Error: Anyone planning to go on the trip should bring the necessary items. Such as a backpack, boots, a canteen, and bug spray.

Problem: The second word group is a phrase and cannot stand alone because it lacks both a subject and a verb. The fragment can be corrected by adding the phrase to the sentence.

Correction: *Anyone planning to go on the trip should bring the necessary items, such as a backpack, boots, a canteen, and bug spray.*

Comma splices appear when two sentences are joined by only a comma. **Run-on sentences** appear when two sentences are run together with no punctuation at all.

Error: Dr. Sanders is a brilliant scientist, his research on genetic disorders won him a Nobel Prize.

Problem: A comma alone cannot join two independent clauses (complete sentences). It must be followed by a coordinating conjunction. The two clauses can be joined by a semi-colon, or they can be separated by a period.

Correction: Dr. Sanders is a brilliant scientist, **and** his research on genetic disorders won him a Nobel Prize.

OR

Dr. Sanders is a brilliant scientist; his research on genetic disorders won him a Nobel Prize.

OR

Dr. Sanders is a brilliant scientist. His research on genetic disorders won him a Nobel Prize.

Standard verb forms

Past tense and past participles
Both regular and irregular verbs must appear in their standard forms for each tense. Note: the -*ed* or -*d* ending is added to regular verbs in the past tense and for past participles.

Infinitive	Past Tense	Past Participle
Bake	Baked	Baked

Irregular Verb Forms

Infinitive	Past Tense	Past Participle
Be	Was, were	Been
Become	Became	Become
Break	Broke	Broken
Bring	Brought	Brought
Choose	Chose	Chosen
Come	Came	Come
Do	Did	Done
Draw	Drew	Drawn
Eat	Ate	Eaten
Fall	Fell	Fallen
Forget	Forgot	Forgotten
Freeze	Froze	Frozen
Give	Gave	Given
Go	Went	Gone
Grow	Grew	Grown
Have/has	Had	Had
Hide	Hid	Hidden
Know	Knew	Known
Lay	Laid	Laid
Lie	Lay	Lain
Ride	Rode	Ridden
Rise	Rose	Risen
Run	Ran	Run
See	Saw	Seen
Steal	Stole	Stolen
Take	Took	Taken
Tell	Told	Told
Throw	Threw	Thrown
Wear	Wore	Worn
Write	Wrote	Written

Error: She should have went to her doctor's appointment at the scheduled time.

Problem: The past participle of the verb *to go* is *gone*. *Went* expresses the simple past tense.

Correction: *She should have gone to her doctor's appointment at the scheduled time.*

Error: My train is suppose to arrive before two o'clock.

Problem: The verb following *train* is a present tense passive construction which requires the present tense verb *to be* and the past participle.

Correction: *My train is supposed to arrive before two o'clock.*

Error: Linda should of known that the car wouldn't start after leaving it out in the cold all night.

Problem: *Should of* is a nonstandard expression. *Of* is not a verb.

Correction: *Linda should have known that the car wouldn't start after leaving it out in the cold all night.*

Inappropriate shifts in verb tense

Verb tenses must refer to the same time period consistently, unless a change in time is required.

Error: Despite the increased number of students in the school this year, overall attendance is higher last year at the sporting events.

Problem: The verb *is* represents an inconsistent shift to the present tense when the action refers to a past occurrence.

Correction: *Despite the increased number of students in the school this year, overall attendance was higher last year at sporting events.*

Error: My friend Lou, who just competed in the marathon, ran since he was twelve years old.

Problem: Because Lou continues to run, the present perfect tense is needed.

Correction: *My friend Lou, who just competed in the marathon, **has run** since he was twelve years old.*

Error: The Mayor congratulated Wallace Mangham, who renovates the city hall last year.

Problem: Although the speaker is talking in the present, the action of renovating the city hall was in the past.

Correction: *The Mayor congratulated Wallace Mangham, who renovated the city hall last year.*

Agreement between subject and verb

A verb must correspond in the singular or plural form with the simple subject; it is not affected by any interfering elements. Note: A simple subject is never found in a prepositional phrase (a phrase beginning with a word such as of, by, over, through, until).

Present Tense Verb Form

	Singular	Plural
1st person (talking about oneself)	I do	We do
2nd person (talking to another)	You do	You do
3rd person (talking about someone or something)	He She does It	They do

Error: Sally, as well as her sister, plan to go into nursing.

Problem: The subject in the sentence is *Sally* alone, not the word *sister*. Therefore, the verb must be singular.

Correction: *Sally, as well as her sister, plans to go into nursing.*

Error: There has been many car accidents lately on that street.

Problem: The subject *accidents* in this sentence is plural; the verb must be plural also --even though it comes before the subject.

Correction: *There have been many car accidents lately on that street.*

Error: Every one of us have a reason to attend the school musical.

Problem: The simple subject is the word *one*, not the *us* in the prepositional phrase. Therefore, the verb must be singular also.

Correction: *Every one of us has a reason to attend the school musical.*

Error: Either the police captain or his officers is going to the convention.

Problem: In either/or and neither/nor constructions, the verb agrees with the subject closer to it.

Correction: *Either the police captain or his officers are going to the convention.*

Agreements between pronoun and antecedent

A pronoun must correspond to its antecedent in number (singular or plural), person (first, second, or third person) and gender (male, female, or neuter). A pronoun must refer clearly to a single word, not to a complete idea.

A **pronoun shift** is a grammatical error in which the author starts a sentence, paragraph, or section of a paper using one particular type of pronoun and then suddenly shifts to another. This often confuses the reader.

Error: A teacher should treat all of their students fairly.

Problem: Since *teacher* is singular, the pronoun referring to it must also be singular. Otherwise, the noun has to be made plural.

Correction: *Teachers should treat all of their students fairly.*

Error: When an actor is rehearsing for a play, it often helps if you can memorize the lines in advance.

Problem: *Actor* is a third-person word; that is, the writer is talking about the subject. The pronoun *you* is in the second person, which means the writer is talking to the subject.

Correction: *When actors are rehearsing for plays, it helps if they can memorize the lines in advance.*

Error: The workers in the factory were upset when his or her paychecks didn't arrive on time.

Problem: *Workers* is a plural form, while *his or her* refers to one person.

Correction: *The workers in the factory were upset when their paychecks didn't arrive on time.*

Error: The charity auction was highly successful, which pleased everyone.

Problem: In this sentence, the pronoun *which* refers to the idea of the auction's success. In fact, *which* has no antecedent in the sentence; the word success is not stated.

Correction: *Everyone was pleased at the success of the auction.*

Clear pronoun references

Rules for clearly identifying pronoun reference

Make sure that the antecedent reference is clear--that the pronoun cannot refer to something else
A "distant relative" is a relative pronoun or a relative clause that has been placed too far away from the antecedent to which it refers. It is a common error to place a verb or a prepositional phrase between a relative pronoun and its antecedent.

Error: Return the books **to the library** that are overdue.
Problem: The relative clause *that are overdue* refers to the *books* and should be placed immediately after **books**.

Correction: Return the books that are overdue to the library.
                Or
            Return the overdue books to the library.

A pronoun should not refer to adjectives or possessive nouns

Adjectives, nouns, or possessive pronouns should not be used as antecedents. This will create ambiguity in sentences.

Error: In Todd's letter, he told his mom that he'd broken the priceless vase.
Problem: In this sentence the pronoun "he" has no antecedent; though it was probably meant to refer to the possessive noun "Todd's."
Correction: In his letter, Todd told his mom that he had broken the priceless vase.

A pronoun should not refer to an implied idea

A pronoun must refer to a specific antecedent rather than to an implied antecedent. When an antecedent is not stated specifically, the reader has to guess or assume the meaning of a sentence. Pronouns that do not have antecedents are called expletives. "It" and "there" are the most common expletives, though other pronouns can also become expletives as well. In informal conversation, expletives allow for a casual presentation of ideas without supporting evidence. However, in more formal writing, it is best to be more precise.

Error: She said that it is important to floss every day.
Problem: The pronoun "it" refers to an implied idea.
Correction: She said that flossing every day is important.

Error: They returned the book because there were missing pages.
Problem: The pronoun "there" does not have a specific antecedent.
Correction: They returned the book because it had missing pages.

Using Who, That and Which

Who, whom and **whose** refer to human beings and can either introduce essential or nonessential clauses. **That** refers to things other than humans and is used to introduce essential clauses. **Which** refers to things other than humans and is used to introduce nonessential clauses.

Error: The doctor that performed the surgery said the man would be fully recovered.

Problem: Since the relative pronoun is referring to a human, who should be used.

Correction: The doctor who performed the surgery said the man would be fully recovered.

Error: That ice cream cone that you just ate looked really delicious.

Problem: *That* has already been used so you must use *which* to introduce the next clause, whether it is essential or nonessential.

Correction: That ice cream cone, which you just ate, looked really delicious.

Proper case forms

Pronouns, unlike nouns, change case forms. Pronouns must be in the subjective, objective, or possessive form according to their function in any given sentence.

Personal Pronouns

	Subjective (Nominative)		Possessive		Objective	
	Singular	Plural	Singular	Plural	Singular	Plural
1st person	I	We	My	Our	Me	Us
2nd person	You	You	Your	Your	You	You
3rd person	He She It	They	His Her Its	Their	Him Her It	Them

Relative Pronouns

Who	Subjective/Nominative
Whom	Objective
Whose	Possessive

Error:	Tom and me have reserved seats for next week's baseball game.
Problem:	The pronoun *me* is the subject of the verb *have reserved* and should be in the nominative, or subject, form.
Correction:	*Tom and I have reserved seats for next week's baseball game.*
Error:	Mr. Green showed all of we students how to make paper hats.
Problem:	The pronoun *we* is the object of the preposition *of*. It should be in the objective form, *us*.
Correction:	*Mr. Green showed all of us students how to make paper hats.*

Error: Who's coat is this?

Problem: The interrogative possessive pronoun is *whose*; *who's* is the contraction for *who is*.

Correction: *Whose coat is this?*

Error: The voters will choose the candidate whom has the best qualifications for the job.

Problem: The case of the relative pronoun *who* or *whom* is determined by the pronoun's function in the clause in which it occurs. The word *who* is in the nominative case, and *whom* is in the objective case. Analyze how the pronoun is being used within the sentence.

Correction: *The voters will choose the candidate who has the best qualifications for the job.*

Identify the correct use of adjectives and adverbs

Adjectives are words that modify or describe nouns or pronouns. Adjectives usually precede the words they modify, but not always; for example, an adjective can occur after a linking verb.

Adverbs are words that modify verbs, adjectives, or other adverbs. They cannot modify nouns. Adverbs answer such questions as how, why, when, where, how much, or how often something is done. Many adverbs are formed by adding *-ly*.

Error: The birthday cake tasted sweetly.

Problem: *Tasted* is a linking verb; the modifier that follows should be an adjective, not an adverb.

Correction: *The birthday cake tasted sweet.*

Error: You have done good with this project.

Problem: *Good* is an adjective or a noun and cannot be used to modify a verb phrase such as *have done*.

Correction: *You have done well with this project.*

Error: The coach was positive happy about the team's chance of winning.

Problem: The adjective *positive* cannot be used to modify another adjective, *happy*. An adverb is needed instead.

Correction: *The coach was positively happy about the team's chance of winning.*

Error: The fireman acted quick and brave to save the child from the burning building.

Problem: *Quick and brave* are adjectives and cannot be used to describe a verb. Adverbs are needed instead.

Correction: *The fireman acted quickly and bravely to save the child from the burning building.*

Appropriate comparative and superlative degree forms

When comparisons are made, the correct form of the adjective or adverb must be used. The comparative form is used for two items. The superlative form is used for more than two.

	Comparative	Superlative
slow	slower	slowest
young	younger	youngest
tall	taller	tallest
quiet	quieter	quiestest
quick	quicker	quickest

With some words, *more* and *most* are used to make comparisons instead of *er* and *est*.

	Comparative	Superlative
energetic	more energetic	most energetic
quickly	more quickly	most quickly

Comparisons must be made between similar structures or items. In the sentence, "My house is similar in color to Steve's," one house is being compared to another house, as conveyed by the use of the possessive *Steve's*.

On the other hand, if the sentence reads "My house is similar in color to Steve," the comparison would be faulty because it would be comparing the house to Steve, not to Steve's house.

Error: Last year's rides at the carnival were bigger than this year.

Problem: In the sentence as it is worded above, the rides at the carnival are being compared to this year, not to this year's rides.

Correction: *Last year's rides at the carnival were bigger than this year's.*

Standard punctuation

Commas

Commas indicate a brief pause. They are used to set off dependent clauses and long introductory word groups, to separate words in a series, to set off unimportant material that interrupts the flow of the sentence, and to separate independent clauses joined by conjunctions.

Error: After I finish my master's thesis I plan to work in Chicago.

Problem: A comma is needed after an introductory, dependent word-group containing a subject and verb.

Correction: *After I finish my master's thesis, I plan to work in Chicago.*

Error: I washed waxed and vacuumed my car today.

Problem: Nouns, phrases, or clauses in a list and two or more coordinate adjectives that modify one word should be separated by commas. Although the word *and* is sometimes considered optional, it is often necessary to clarify the meaning.

Correction: *I washed, waxed, and vacuumed my car today.*

Error: She was a talented dancer but she is mostly remembered for her singing ability.

Problem: A comma is needed before a conjunction that joins two independent clauses (complete sentences).

Correction: *She was a talented dancer, but she is mostly remembered for her singing ability.*

Error: This incident is I think typical of what can happen when the community remains so divided.

Problem: Commas are needed between nonessential words or words that interrupt the main clause.

Correction: *This incident is, I think, typical of what can happen when the community remains so divided.*

Semicolons and colons

Semicolons are needed to separate two or more closely related independent clauses when the second clause is introduced by a transitional adverb. (These clauses may also be written as separate sentences, preferably by placing the adverb within the second sentence).

Colons are used to introduce lists and to emphasize what follows.

Error: I climbed to the top of the mountain, it took me three hours.

Problem: A comma alone cannot separate two independent clauses. Instead a semicolon is needed to separate two related sentences.

Correction: *I climbed to the top of the mountain; it took me three hours.*

Error: In the movie, asteroids destroyed Dallas, Texas, Kansas City, Missouri, and Boston, Massachusetts.

Problem: Semicolons are needed to separate items in a series that already contains internal punctuation.

Correction: *In the movie, asteroids destroyed Dallas, Texas; Kansas City, Missouri; and Boston, Massachusetts.*

Error: Essays will receive the following grades, A for excellent, B for good, C for average, and D for unsatisfactory.

Problem: A colon is needed to emphasize the information or list that follows.

Correction: *Essays will receive the following grades: A for excellent, B for good, C for average, and D for unsatisfactory.*

Error: The school carnival included: amusement rides, clowns, food booths, and a variety of games.

Problem: The material preceding the colon and the list that follows is not a complete sentence. Do not separate a verb (or preposition) from the object.

Correction: *The school carnival included amusement rides, clowns, food booths, and a variety of games.*

Apostrophes

Apostrophes are used to form contractions, to indicate possession, and, rarely, to form plurals.

Error: She shouldnt be permitted to smoke cigarettes in the building.

Problem: An apostrophe is needed in a contraction in place of the missing letter.

Correction: *She shouldn't be permitted to smoke cigarettes in the building.*

Error: My cousins motorcycle was stolen from his driveway.

Problem: An apostrophe is needed to show possession.

Correction: *My cousin's motorcycle was stolen from his driveway.* (Note: The use of the apostrophe before the letter "s" means that there is just one cousin. The plural form would read the following way: My cousins' motorcycle was stolen from their driveway.)

Error: The childrens new kindergarten teacher was also a singer.

Problem: An apostrophe is needed to show possession.

Correction: *The children's new kindergarten teacher was also a singer.* (Note: Children is plural)

Quotation marks

In a quoted statement that is either declarative or imperative, place the period inside the closing quotation marks.

"The airplane crashed on the runway during takeoff."

If the quotation is followed by other words in the sentence, place a comma inside the closing quotations marks and a period at the end of the sentence.

"The airplane crashed on the runway during takeoff," said the announcer.

In most instances in which a quoted title or expression occurs at the end of a sentence, the period is placed before either the single or double quotation marks.

"The middle school readers were unprepared to understand Bryant's poem 'Thanatopsis.'"

Early book-length adventure stories like *Don Quixote* and *The Three Musketeers* were known as "picaresque novels."

In sentences that are interrogatory or exclamatory, the question mark or exclamation point should be positioned outside the closing quotation marks if the quote itself is a statement or command or cited title.

Who decided to lead us in the recitation of the "Pledge of Allegiance"?

Why was Tillie shaking as she began her recitation, "Once upon a midnight dreary..."?

I was embarrassed when Mrs. White said, "Your slip is showing"!

In sentences that are declarative, but the quotation is a question or an exclamation, place the question mark or exclamation point inside the quotation marks.

The hall monitor yelled, "Fire! Fire!"

"Fire! Fire!" yelled the hall monitor.

Cory shrieked, "Is there a mouse in the room?" (In this instance, the question supersedes the exclamation.)

Quotations - whether words, phrases, or clauses - should be punctuated according to the rules of the grammatical function they serve in the sentence.

> The works of Shakespeare, "the Bard of Avon," have been contested as originating with other authors.

> "You'll get my money," the old man warned, "when Hell freezes over."

> Sheila cited the passage that began "Four score and seven years ago...." (Note the ellipsis followed by an enclosed period.)

> "Old Ironsides" inspired the preservation of the U.S.S. Constitution.

Use quotation marks to enclose the titles of shorter works: songs, short poems, short stories, essays, and chapters of books. (See "Using Italics" for punctuating longer titles.)

> "The Tell-Tale Heart"   "Casey at the Bat"   "America the Beautiful"

Dashes and Italics

Place **dashes** to denote sudden breaks in thought.

> Some periods in literature - the Romantic Age, for example - spanned different time periods in different countries.

Use dashes instead of commas if commas are already used elsewhere in the sentence for amplification or explanation.

> The Fireside Poets included three Brahmans - James Russell Lowell, Henry David Wadsworth, Oliver Wendell Holmes - and John Greenleaf Whittier.

Use **italics** to punctuate the titles of long works of literature; names of periodical publications; musical scores; works of art; and motion picture television, and radio programs. (When unable to write in italics, students should be instructed to underline in their own writing where italics would be appropriate.)

> *The Idylls of the King*   *Hiawatha*   *The Sound and the Fury*
> *Mary Poppins*   *Newsweek*   *The Nutcracker Suite*

Standard capitalization

Capitalize all proper names of persons (including specific organizations or agencies of government); places (countries, states, cities, parks, and specific geographical areas); and things (political parties, structures, historical and cultural terms, and calendar and time designations); and religious terms (any deity, revered person or group, and sacred writings).

> Percy Bysshe Shelley, Argentina, Mount Rainier National Park, the Grand Canyon, League of Nations, the Sears Tower, Birmingham, Lyric Theater, Americans, Midwesterners, Democrats, Renaissance, Boy Scouts of America, Easter, God, Bible, Dead Sea Scrolls, Koran

Capitalize proper adjectives and titles used with proper names.

California gold rush, President John Adams, French fries, Homeric epic, Romanesque architecture, Senator John Glenn

Note: Some words that represent titles and offices are not capitalized unless used with a proper name.

Capitalized	Not Capitalized
Congressman McKay	the congressman from California
Commander Alger	commander of the Pacific Fleet
Queen Elizabeth	the queen of England

Capitalize all main words in titles of works of literature, art, and music.

Error: Emma went to Dr. Peters for treatment since her own Doctor was on vacation.

Problem: The use of capital letters with Emma and Dr. Peters is correct since they are specific (proper) names; the title Dr. is also capitalized. However, the word doctor is not a specific name and should not be capitalized.

Correction: *Emma went to Dr. Peters for treatment since her own doctor was on vacation.*

Error: Our Winter Break does not start until next Wednesday.

Problem: Days of the week are capitalized, but seasons are not capitalized.

Correction: *Our winter break does not start until next Wednesday.*

Error: The exchange student from israel who came to study biochemistry spoke spanish very well.

Problem: Languages and the names of countries are always capitalized. Courses are also capitalized when they refer to a specific course; they are not capitalized when they refer to courses in general.

Correction: *The exchange student from Israel who came to study Biochemistry spoke Spanish very well.*

XAMonline, INC. 21 Orient Ave. Melrose, MA 02176

Toll Free number 800-509-4128

TO ORDER Fax 781-662-9268 OR www.XAMonline.com

CALIFORNIA SUBJECT EXAMINATIONS   - CSET - 2008

PO#   Store/School:

Address 1:

Address 2 (Ship to other):

City, State Zip

Credit card number_____-_____-_____-_____   expiration_____

EMAIL _____

PHONE   **FAX**

ISBN	TITLE	Qty	Retail	Total
978-1-58197-595-6	RICA Reading Instruction Competence Assessment			
978-1-58197-596-3	CBEST CA Basic Educational Skills			
978-1-58197-901-5	CSET French Sample Test 149, 150			
978-1-58197-622-9	CSET Spanish 145, 146, 147			
978-1-58197-803-2	CSET MSAT Multiple Subject 101, 102, 103			
978-1-58197-261-0	CSET English 105, 106, 107			
978-1-58197-608-3	CSET Foundational-Level Mathematics 110, 111			
978-1-58197-285-6	CSET Mathematics 110, 111, 112			
978-1-58197-340-2	CSET Social Science 114, 115			
978-1-58197-342-6	CSET General Science 118, 119			
978-1-58197-809-4	CSET Biology-Life Science 120, 124			
978-1-58197-395-2	CSET Chemistry 121, 125			
978-1-58197-571-0	CSET Earth and Planetary Science 122, 126			
978-1-58197-817-9	CSET Physics 123, 127			
978-1-58197-299-3	CSET Physical Education, 129, 130, 131			
978-1-58197-813-1	CSET Art Sample Subtest 140			
			SUBTOTAL	
			Ship	$8.70
			TOTAL	

CPSIA information can be obtained at www.ICGtesting.com
Printed in the USA
LVOW021505230911

247590LV00004B/40/P